THE

VEGETARIAN

CHILI

COOKBOOK

THE VEGETARIAN CHILI COOKBOOK

80 Deliciously Different One-Dish Meals

ROBIN ROBERTSON

THE HARVARD COMMON PRESS
Boston, Massachusetts

The Harvard Common Press
535 Albany Street
Boston, Massachusetts 02118

Printed in the United States of America
Printed on acid-free paper

Library of Congress Cataloging-in-Publication Data

Robertson, Robin (Robin G.)
    The vegetarian chili cookbook : 80 deliciously different one-dish meals /
by Robin Robertson.
        p.   cm.
    Includes index.
        ISBN 1-55832-147-0 (hbk. : alk. paper). — ISBN 1-55832-148-9 (pbk. :
alk paper)
        1. Vegetarian cookery.   2. Chili con carne.   I. Title.
    TX837.R626   1998
    641.8'23—dc21   98-35574
                                                                                                        CIP

Special bulk-order discounts are available on this and other Harvard Common
Press books. Companies and organizations may purchase books for premiums
or resale, or may arrange a custom edition, by contacting the Marketing
Director at the address above.

Cover and book illustrations by Brooke Scudder
Cover and book design by Kathleen Herlihy-Paoli, Inkstone Design

THIS BOOK IS DEDICATED TO *AHIMSA*.

CONTENTS

● ● ●

Acknowledgments

I'D LIKE TO EXPRESS MY HEARTFELT THANKS TO MY HUSBAND, JON ROBERTSON, FOR HIS TIRELESS HOURS OF TASTING, TESTING, AND COMPUTER HELP — ALONG WITH MY ETERNAL GRATITUDE THAT HE JUST HAPPENS TO LOVE CHILI; TO MY FRIEND JUNE ROBBINS, FOR HER MORAL SUPPORT AND HELP WITH THE TASTING AND TESTING; TO MY FRIEND SANTI MEUNIER, FOR SHARING; TO MY EDITOR, DAN ROSENBERG, FOR HIS VISION AND DEDICATION TO THIS PROJECT; AND TO THE ENTIRE STAFF AT THE HARVARD COMMON PRESS FOR THEIR HELP AND ENTHUSIASM.

THE
VEGETARIAN
CHILI
COOKBOOK

INTRODUCTION

Nothing beats a hearty "bowl of red." Chili is the all-American favorite, that robust one-dish meal that falls somewhere between a soup and a stew. It's delicious, simple to make, economical, and easy to freeze and store.

What makes chili *chili*? Chili aficionados are zealous about what they consider to be authentic chili. Indeed, to some, the art of making and eating chili is almost a religious experience. There are those who insist that chili contain no beans. Others say no beans and no tomatoes, only meat and spices. With that said, my desire to write an entirely vegetarian chili book may be considered heresy in some circles, but as a chili lover and a vegetarian, I feel it's time to bridge the gap.

Chili is typically said to have originated with Texas trail cooks in the 1800s, with classic Texas Chili reverently prepared with bite-sized chunks of meat instead of ground beef. However, nearly every region in the United States has its own indigenous chili tradition: Five-Way Cincinnati Chili is served with layers of spaghetti, chili, beans, onions, and cheese. In New Mexico, chili is served with beans on the side. In Kansas City, chili is often mixed with macaroni in a casserole and called "chili-mac." Some regional chili recipes include such diverse ingredients as beer, coffee, allspice, or chocolate. Depending upon where you live, toppings can include chopped onions, grated cheese, sour cream, or diced avocado.

Most vegetarian cookbooks are limited to a handful of chili recipes, and most chili cookbooks rarely include more than a single vegetarian recipe, despite the fact that many who practice "heart smart" cooking are searching for that perfect vegetarian chili recipe as a delicious way to reduce their meat intake. Given the availability of excellent meat alternatives made from vegetable and grain proteins (see pages 11–14), and the proliferation of exciting "fusion" foods, vegetarians and meat-eaters alike owe it to themselves to expand their chili horizons.

While sifting through all the varied definitions pre-

ferred by chili-heads, I noted some observations: Chili most closely resembles a stew in appearance and preparation. It is typically hearty and substantial. What differentiates it from other stews is that it always contains some form of chile pepper, usually in the form of chili powder; some kind of meat; and the seasonings cumin and oregano. And chili often contains tomatoes, beans, onions, and garlic.

Chili enthusiasts devour the dish mild, hot, or super-hot, often armed with little more than a few crackers and a lot of intestinal fortitude. Although tradition dictates that chili be served in a bowl and eaten with a spoon, it can be ladled thick over noodles, rice, or cornbread.

In this book I make liberal use of traditional chili beans—kidneys and pintos—but I venture into other bean varieties as well, including lentils, chickpeas, favas, and cannellinis. Instead of ground meat, these recipes rely on a tasty selection of meat alternatives such as seitan, tempeh, or textured soy protein to give meatless chili that familiar "meaty" texture. It is my feeling that the meat used in chili, whether animal or vegetable, serves as the vehicle or conveyance of the other chili seasonings and ingredients while adding texture and substance to the dish.

In addition to recipes that offer alternatives to meat, the book contains a variety of intriguing, uniquely vegetarian chili recipes that feature corn, eggplant, fennel, and other delicious gifts of nature from avocados to zucchini. There are also international chili variations, fragrant with heady seasonings like ginger, curry, and hoisin sauce.

Meatless chili is a persuasive ambassador for vegetarianism because it's perfect for casual family dinners and parties alike, pleasing everyone from vegan to meat-eater. It makes a great "first dish" to serve to someone new to vegetarian cuisine. In an age when more and more people are choosing vegetarianism, the chili recipes in this book will help take the guesswork out of entertaining. And since chili tastes even better reheated, it's an ideal "make-ahead" dish for busy weekday meals or informal gatherings.

CHILI TRADITIONS AND LORE

A Chili State of Mind

"The beauty of chili to me is that it's really a state of mind. It's what you want when you make it. You can put anything in there you want, make it hot or mild, any blend of spices you feel like at the time. You make it up to suit your mood."
—CARROLL SHELBY, quoted in *The International Chili Society's Official Chili Cookbook*

Chili, like politics or religion, is a controversial subject, and as many stories surround its origins as there are recipe variations. One legend attributes its beginnings to a seventeenth-century Spanish nun: While in a trance, the nun is said to have seen a vision of Indians in the American Southwest eating chili; apparently, she wrote down the recipe afterward. Some say chili originated as Texas prison food in the 1800s. Others who claim to have had a hand in its origin include both Irish and Chinese chuckwagon cooks, American Indians, Confederate officers, and the Magyars. The most widely accepted legend traces its beginnings to nineteenth-century Texans, who invented it as a trail-side meal during the California gold rush of the 1850s by using readily available ingredients: the indigenous chile peppers and the ubiquitous beef.

During chili's infancy during the mid-1800s, another chili phenomenon emerged, in San Antonio, in the guise of "chili queens"—women who set up stands or booths in the plaza to sell chili to soldiers passing through. These chili queens remained popular for quite some time and may be among the first outdoor food vendors in the United States.

Chili grew in popularity not only across Texas but throughout the United States, and by the twentieth century eateries known as "chili parlors" dotted the landscape, and recipe variations abounded. Its popularity spread after it was introduced to the country at the St. Louis World's Fair in 1904. Chili was declared the official state dish of Texas in 1977, and today is hailed by many as America's favorite meal. International chili organizations, complete with newsletters and cook-offs, give rise to still more variety, lore, and debate.

Chili cook-offs are held in virtually every part of the United States—at state fairs, civic clubs, firehouses, church halls, and rodeos. They can be small, friendly gatherings or massive, fierce competitions. Some have been held for specific groups—"women only," those of Japanese descent, service-

men, or those who are handicapped, to cite just a few. There are several annual vegetarian chili cook-offs, usually sponsored by regional vegetarian organizations. I know of no other dish that inspires as much interest, enthusiasm, and controversy as chili.

The main chili debate tends to focus on ingredients: primarily, whether to add beans, and, if so, what kind. Should chili contain tomatoes, or any vegetables? Should the consistency be thick, or thin? Since a vegetarian chili cookbook is in itself an aberration to most chili purists, I have decided to create a chili book where truly anything (except meat) may turn up in a recipe—as long as it is tasty and can fit into the other criteria set forth in our definition of chili.

There is a question regarding the correct way to spell the word *chili*. First of all, a *chile*, or chile "pepper," is not really a pepper at all; it's a capsicum. However, since Columbus first misnamed them, chiles have been dubbed "peppers." To add to the confusion, the capsicum is sometimes spelled *chili*, the same as its stew-like namesake.

For the purposes of this book, *chili* is the dish and *chili powder* is the pre-mixed blend of seasonings. *Chiles* are the "peppers"—the pods or fruits of the capsicum plant—and *ground chiles* are the pure ground dried chiles with no other ingredients blended in.

ALL ABOUT CHILES

There are hundreds of varieties of chiles, ranging from mildly sweet to searingly hot. Many are available fresh or dried. Fresh unripe chiles are green, with a sharper flavor, and the ripe red chiles have a fuller, more robust flavor. Generally speaking, the larger the chile, the milder it will be. The mainstay of chili powder is the ground dried red chile. However it can be fun to experiment by adding some fresh varieties to the pot. Some people don't like the raw taste they say fresh chiles add to the flavor, and prefer to stick with the traditional dried, while others disagree wholeheartedly. As with most everything else about chili, settling the fresh-versus-dried controversy is best left to individual taste. These days many supermarkets carry a selection of both fresh and dried chiles, so experimenting can be part of the overall chili adventure.

Among the most popular chiles used in chili-making are the Anaheim, the ancho, and the jalapeño. The Anaheim is about five inches long and two to three inches wide, with a pointed tip, and is green or red in color. The ancho is similar in size and shape to a bell pepper—broad and wide. In the United States, anchos are available dried, and they are usually a deep reddish brown. Oftentimes, the ancho is blended with the mild Anaheim to make chili powder. Ground dried cayenne or some other hot chile can be added to turn up the heat.

Another popular way to add a fiery punch to chili is by adding the jalapeño. Jalapeños are dark green, about two inches in length and one inch in diameter. They're available fresh or canned in most supermarkets. Before using, they should be stemmed, seeded, deveined, and minced fine. In its dried state, the jalapeño is called a chipotle. Other hot chiles include the serrano, cascabel, habanero or Scotch Bonnet, and the tiny chiltepin. These chiles are not for the faint of heart and should be used with extreme caution. In addition to heat, the many chile varieties provide their own unique flavors, making them a tempting ingredient for the adventuresome cook.

When handling chiles, it is best to wear rubber gloves. Be careful not to touch your eyes because the capsaicin oil will burn. Some of the hotter chiles even release fumes that are quite strong. Always wash your hands and gloves in warm soapy water after handling chiles.

Alternate heat sources for chili recipes include prepared salsa and hot pepper sauces such as Tabasco, Louisiana hot sauce, or any of the myriad of hot sauces—with colorful names like "The Devil's Mouthwash" to extol their fiery nature—widely available in supermarkets.

CHILI POWDER AND CHILI SPICES

Chile Fact

Chile molido *refers to pure ground chile without added spices.*

There are different ways to achieve the unmistakable flavor of chili. The easiest and most common way is to use one of those pre-blended commercial chili powders. You can make your own chili powder blend with already ground dried chiles, or dried chiles that you can grind yourself and then customize by adding cumin and other seasonings such as oregano and paprika.

Commercially available chili powders are generally a blend of ground chile peppers combined with cumin, oregano, garlic, and salt. These blends can vary greatly in quality and flavor and can sometimes be stale or of inferior quality. When you use a particular brand of chili powder, you are only experiencing that company's notion of what chili seasoning should taste like. In a pinch, of course, a good quality chili powder can be a godsend when you crave that "bowl of blessedness," as the great American humorist Will Rogers affectionately dubbed chili.

In selecting a commercial powder blend, try to find one that consists only of ground chiles, oregano, and cumin. For the best flavor, try to steer clear of those containing garlic, salt, and other additives. For my taste, the flavor of fresh garlic is far superior to powdered, and I think it's best to be in control of how much salt goes into the pot. Additives can include sugar, monosodium glutamate, tapioca starch, whey, lactose, and food coloring. I'll have mine without, thanks.

There are other commercial chili powders that are called "kits" or "fixin's." These products generally contain small packets of the individual seasonings allowing you to create your own combination. This type of product offers you the convenience of commercial chili powders while giving you some control over the actual mix. Wick Fowler's 2-Alarm Chili Kit and Carroll Shelby's Original Texas Brand Chili Mix are two brands available in most supermarkets. If you want to experience the true flavors of chiles in all their variety, how-

ever, you may want to create your own blend.

The following recipes are for three of my favorite blends; you can use them any time a recipe calls for "chili powder," as your preference for hot or mild dictates. Although the first two recipes start with dried whole chiles that you grind yourself, you may substitute already ground chiles, which are often sold simply as "hot" or "mild." The third recipe begins with ground ingredients. It is a predominantly mild blend with just a touch of heat. To increase the heat, add more hot ground chiles to the mixture.

Hot Chili Powder

Use this as a guideline and experiment with different types and amounts of chiles to create your own signature blend.

> *2 dried cayenne chiles, stems and seeds removed*
> *4 dried ancho chiles, stems and seeds removed*
> *1 tablespoon cumin seeds*
> *1 teaspoon dried oregano, preferably Mexican*

Cut the chiles into small pieces and place in a blender or spice mill, along with the cumin seeds and oregano. Grind into a fine powder. Store in an airtight container in a cool, dry place.

Mild Chili Powder

The coriander adds a spicy, sweet touch, and the paprika intensifies the powder's reddish color. As with the hot chili powder, you can vary the ingredients to create your own blend.

>   *3 dried ancho chiles, stems and seeds removed*
>   *3 dried Anaheim chiles, stems and seeds removed*
>   *1 tablespoon cumin seeds*
>   *1 tablespoon paprika*
>   *1 teaspoon dried oregano, preferably Mexican*
>   *½ teaspoon coriander seeds*

Cut the chiles into small pieces and place in a blender or spice mill with the cumin, paprika, oregano, and coriander. Grind into a fine powder. Store in an airtight container in a cool, dry place.

Mostly Mild Chili Powder

Mostly mild, this blend can easily be made hot by increasing the amount of hot ground chiles. The cumin and oregano amounts may be adjusted as well.

>   *1 cup mild ground dried chiles*
>   *¼ cup hot ground dried chiles*
>   *2 tablespoons ground cumin*
>   *2 tablespoons ground oregano, preferably Mexican*

Combine all ingredients together, mixing well. Store in an airtight container in a cool, dry place.

The type and amount of spices that go into your chili is a matter of personal taste. In this book, I delve into a wide variety of seasoning combinations. I prefer using Mexican oregano, because I find it to be more flavorful than European

oregano, but it's not a necessary requirement for making a great pot of chili, and the European variety will suffice. If you'd like to experiment with Mexican oregano, look for it in the international section of your supermarket, specialty stores, or mail-order catalogs.

You may notice that some recipes call for extra cumin, oregano, or other spices in addition to the specified chili powder blend. However, if you're not particularly fond of cumin, for example, you may choose to simply omit any added cumin from your recipe and the chili will still taste fine. Always remember that less is more. If you're not sure how well you like a spice, or how hot you want the dish, season it a little at a time—you can always add more, but you can't take it back once it goes in. In addition to chili powder, some recipes call for minced fresh chiles, which can give an added dimension of flavor, and often heat, to a pot of chili. Remember that while chili tastes better a day or two later, those spices also intensify over time.

To Bean or Not To Bean

A majority of the recipes in this book call for beans of one kind or another. Many people prefer to cook with dried beans, whereas others enjoy the convenience of canned beans, even though they may contain large amounts of sodium. In any case, when beans are used in chili, they are best cooked ahead of time—the reason my recipes invariably call for "cooked" beans. You can decide how they get that way. If you're using canned beans, you may want to buy one of the organic varieties because they generally contain no additives and very little sodium. Always drain canned beans and rinse them in cold water before using. Typically, a 15-ounce can of beans is equal to one and a half cups in volume.

Dried beans need to be soaked prior to cooking. They can be quick-soaked in a pot of hot, boiled water for an hour,

or left covered in the refrigerator to soak overnight. Do not use salt at the beginning of the cooking process, as this will toughen the beans. I like to add a piece of *kombu* seaweed to the pot when cooking beans: While it won't affect the taste, *kombu* acts as a natural flavor enhancer and tenderizer, helps decrease the cooking time, and aids in digestion.

You may want to consult the chart of beans and cooking times prior to cooking one of the many varieties of beans used in this book.

Bean Cooking Times

(Note: All beans except lentils should be soaked in water overnight or quick-soaked for an hour prior to cooking.)

BEANS	WATER	COOKING TIME	YIELD
(1 cup dry)	(cups)	(hours)	(cups)
Adzuki	3	1	2
Black	4	1 1/2	2
Black-eyed peas	3	1	2
Cannellini	3	1 1/2	2
Chickpeas	4	3	2 1/4
Great Northern	3 1/2	2	2
Kidney	3	2	2
Lentils	3	1	2 1/4
Pinto	3	2	2

WHY MEATLESS?

People everywhere are looking for ways to eat less meat for a variety of reasons, ranging from good health, to ethics, to economics. Whether it is to ward off cardiovascular disease, high cholesterol, cancer, or food poisoning, going meatless seems to be the preferred choice for many people. Medical

Meatless: In Good Company

"Meat is high in cholesterol which clogs up your heart's arteries. Meat is high in saturated fat, which raises your blood cholesterol level. Meat is high in oxidants, like iron, which oxidize cholesterol to a form that is more easily deposited in your arteries. Meat is low in antioxidants."

—DEAN ORNISH, M.D., *Eat More, Weigh Less*

science shows that humankind does not need animal protein to live: In fact, it's the ingestion of animal meat that has been found to be the root cause of much of the heart disease, strokes, and cancer in this country. Therefore, I suggest that the use of typical chili ingredients such as beef, pork, bacon drippings, and lard deserves a second thought from even the most ardent chili purist.

In the United States alone, more than 12 million people consider themselves vegetarians. Many of them "go veggie" because studies have proven that a diet high in vegetables and complex carbohydrates is more healthful. Vegetarians feel better, live longer, and can be confident knowing they are helping themselves, the world's animals, and the environment. Through my experience as a chef, I've been able to demonstrate that most dishes that use meat can be satisfactorily duplicated by correctly using meat alternatives. Vegetarian chili is perhaps the best example of all.

MEAT ALTERNATIVES

Many years ago, when I first attempted a vegetarian diet, the only protein sources available to me were beans and the occasional package of tofu (when I could find it). Try as I might, it was difficult to transform many of my "meat" recipes into meatless versions. These days, however, as vegetarianism becomes more mainstream, a growing selection of vegetable protein options exists. A new generation of meat alternatives has arrived to complement the basic plant-based protein sources of tofu (soybean curd), tempeh (compressed soybeans), seitan (wheat-meat), and textured soy protein, an economical dehydrated product that reconstitutes with water.

The new products, usually a blend of soy and grains, are made to mimic meat in taste and texture and run the gamut from hot dogs, to cold cuts, to sausage. I find these products to be extremely helpful in creative cooking. It's now a simple matter to transform most any "meat" recipe into a healthful meatless version.

Among my favorites are the ground beef substitutes that taste remarkably like ground beef but are low in fat, have no cholesterol, and, of course, contain no gristle, bone, or saturated fat. I especially love them because they're perfect for chili recipes, providing the taste and texture we've come to expect from chili without all the calories, cholesterol, and fat.

Here is a list of common meat alternatives that can be used to make great chili:

GROUND BEEF ALTERNATIVE These vegetable protein crumbles come under a variety of brand names and are available in the freezer sections of many supermarkets and natural foods stores. They have a texture and flavor most like cooked ground beef. Most of them come "precooked" or already browned and ready to use. One brand, Morningstar Farms Burger-Style Recipe Crumbles, is available in many supermarkets, as is Green Giant Harvest Burgers for Recipes. Both come in 12-ounce packages, which is equivalent to one to one and a half pounds of uncooked ground beef. Other brands, such as Tofu Crumbles, may be easier to find in natural foods stores. Other products exist that may need to be cooked briefly before using, so, for the sake of clarity, the recipes in this book specify the use of a "cooked" ground beef alternative and refer to the types of product brands mentioned above.

SEITAN Called "wheat-meat" because it is made from wheat, seitan (pronounced "say-TAN") can be used in virtually any meat recipe, including chili. It can be ground, diced, cubed, or sliced. Made with wheat flour and water, seitan can be purchased in several forms, including a dry "quick mix." Ready-made seitan is also available in jars or in the frozen food or refrigerator sections of most natural foods stores. In addition to being a good source of protein, vitamin C, and iron, seitan is also low in fat and calories: A 4-ounce serving contains only 70 calories and 1 gram of fat.

TEMPEH Tempeh is fermented, compressed soybeans which are formed into firm cakes. Tempeh has a distinctive flavor and

Can Chili Be Low-Fat?

"**H**ealthful chili" is no longer an oxymoron. Traditional chili recipes are awash in saturated fat because they are often started with suet or bacon drippings and they contain all manner of meats. Enter the new breed: vegetarian chili. These recipes call for little more than one tablespoon of oil, and they are chock full of healthful vegetables and beans. Now chili can be a low-fat, high-fiber option that's as good for you as it is good-tasting. These new "virtuous" chili recipes are also quick and easy. Because there are no "cheap cuts" of meat to tenderize, most recipes can be ready in less than an hour.

chewy texture and can be cubed, crumbled, or grated to resemble ground meat for chili. It is high in protein and B-complex vitamins, including vitamin B12. Tempeh can be found in the refrigerator section of natural foods stores and of some supermarkets.

TOFU Tofu is a curd made from soybeans. Its distinct lack of flavor makes tofu a valuable ingredient for the imaginative cook because it readily absorbs other flavors and seasonings. In years past, tofu was one of the few vegetarian protein choices available, but now, with the new meat alternatives in the spotlight, I tend to use tofu more as an egg or dairy substitute (my book *366 Simply Delicious Dairy-free Recipes* is loaded with ideas for its use). Tofu is now made into convincing cheese and sour cream substitutes that can be used as a delicious no-cholesterol chili topping. When using firm tofu as a meat alternative in chili, it is best to press out the water before using. It can then be crumbled and lightly browned. Nutritionally, tofu is very high in protein, calcium, iron, and B-complex vitamins.

TEXTURED SOY PROTEIN Also called texturized vegetable protein, or TVP®, it is made from compressed soy flour to produce dried fibrous granules that can be used in any recipe calling for ground meat. An economical convenience food, textured soy protein reconstitutes easily in equal measure with boiling water or any other liquid, and it is available in granules and chunks. It is packaged under various brand names and is also available in bulk. It can be found in many supermarkets, most natural foods stores, and some mail-order catalogs. Textured soy protein is often used in processed products, where it may be listed as "hydrolyzed vegetable protein" or simply "soy protein." The new breed of ready-to-use products, such as the frozen "burger crumbles," are often more flavorful, but can cost twice as much as the economical dehydrated product. As with anything made from soybeans, textured soy protein is an extremely high source of protein, B-complex vitamins, vitamin A, calcium, and iron.

Just like different cuts of meat, each of these meat alter-

natives lends different subtleties of taste and texture to the chili pot. Seitan, cubed tempeh, and soy protein chunks provide textures similar to tender cubed stew meat. Burger-style "crumbles," textured soy protein granules, crumbled or grated tempeh, and crumbled tofu behave much like ground beef in recipes. By experimenting with combinations, I have chosen what I feel to be the best meat alternative for a particular recipe; however, others may be used to suit individual tastes. I encourage you to experiment, too, and use what you like best.

ABOUT STOCKS AND OILS

As with just about every aspect of chili, the use of stock is a matter of personal taste. My feeling is that since chili itself has so many dominant flavors, the subtle taste of vegetable stock may get "lost in the sauce." However, vegetable stock or broth remains one of the favored alternatives to water in chili, along with beer, red wine, and tomato juice. You can make vegetable stock from scratch, or use canned broth or an instant vegetable base.

To make a basic vegetable stock, heat a small amount of oil in a large stockpot and add one or two each of chopped onions, carrots, and celery ribs, along with other assorted chopped vegetables such as zucchini, potatoes (with peels), garlic, and mushrooms. Cover the pot, and cook the vegetables over medium heat for 5 minutes to bring out the flavor of the vegetables. Add one or two quartered tomatoes, some chopped parsley, and salt and fresh-ground black pepper to taste, along with at least four quarts of water. Bring the mixture to a boil, lower the heat, and simmer, uncovered, until the liquid reduces by half. Strain the stock. Use immediately, or divide into small containers and freeze.

Regarding oils: In the interest of good health, I have considerably reduced the amount of oil typically found in chili recipes. I generally use olive oil to give a chili a Mediterranean

flavor, or, for general use, safflower oil, since it is the lowest in saturated fat of all the cooking oils. You can use a little more oil than is called for, or no oil at all, in which case you'd simply begin your cooking process in a little water to "sweat" the vegetables. Whatever you decide, you'll notice that these grease-free vegetarian chilis are much easier to digest than those made with meat.

THE CARE AND FREEZING OF CHILI

More than with most dishes, the flavor of chili actually improves with age and reheating. As many people do, I prefer to make chili a day in advance so that the flavors will intensify. However, the intoxicating aroma of the simmering chili wafting through the house usually guarantees that some major sampling will take place as soon as it finishes cooking. Chili also freezes well, so plan to make a huge potful and freeze it in batches for a quick meal at a moment's notice. Be sure the chili has cooled completely before sealing it well and then refrigerating or freezing it. Keep in mind that the intensity of the chili spices increases once the chili is stored.

Many chili fanatics have one particular large pot, often an old cast-iron job, that is reserved exclusively as the chili pot. Since many people don't own such a cherished relic, here are some basic guidelines. Look for a pot that is large enough to hold a good batch of chili, with room to spare—at least 4½ to 5 quarts. It should be heavy enough for even heat distribution and be made of a non-reactive material. If you can't find a cast-iron classic, then a good quality stainless steel pot will work just fine. Whether you use a saucepan, stockpot, Dutch oven, or grandma's old soup pot, once you get the chili-making fever, your vessel is destined to become the "chili pot." And, if you're like me, a simmering pot of hearty vegetarian chili will be making regular appearances in your kitchen.

GARDEN VARIETY

WHILE EXPERIMENTING WITH VEGETABLES FOR THIS BOOK, I WAS STRUCK WITH JUST HOW VERSATILE VEGETABLES CAN BE.

THIS CHAPTER CELEBRATES THE ABUNDANT VARIETY AND VERSATILITY OF VEGETABLES WITH A COLLECTION OF DELICIOUS CHILI RECIPES THAT SHOWCASE VEGETABLES AS THE MAIN INGREDIENTS. THESE "VERY VEGGIE" CHILI RECIPES PROVIDE YOU WITH A NEW WAY TO ENJOY FAVORITE VEGETABLES WITHOUT SACRIFICING ALL THE FLAVOR AND SPICINESS OF TRADITIONAL CHILI.

GARDEN VEGETABLE CHILI

THIS CHILI RELIES ON A CORNUCOPIA OF FRESH VEGETABLES FOR ITS TEXTURE AND FLAVOR. IT'S A GREAT WAY TO MAKE SURE EVERYONE "EATS THEIR VEGETABLES."

1 tablespoon safflower oil
1 large onion, chopped
1 large carrot, diced
1 small red bell pepper, diced
½ cup chopped celery
2 garlic cloves, minced
1 jalapeño, seeded and minced
2 small zucchini, diced
2 large tomatoes, chopped
2 cups fresh or frozen corn kernels
2 cups water
1 can (6-ounce) tomato paste
4 tablespoons hot or mild chili powder (pages 7-8)
1 teaspoon salt
1 teaspoon dried oregano, preferably Mexican
1 teaspoon sugar
2 tablespoons minced parsley, for garnish

Heat the oil in a large chili pot over medium heat. Add the onion, carrot, bell pepper, celery, garlic, and jalapeño. Cover, and cook, stirring occasionally, until the vegetables begin to soften, about 10 minutes. Add the zucchini, tomatoes, corn, water, tomato paste, chili powder, salt, oregano, and sugar, and stir well. Bring to a boil, lower the heat, and simmer until the vegetables are tender, about 30 minutes, adding more water if necessary. Serve garnished with the minced parsley.

SERVES 4

PUMPKIN AND BLACK BEAN CHILI

THE VIVID CONTRAST OF THE BLACK BEANS AND BRIGHT ORANGE PUMPKIN MAKES THIS CHILI A PERFECT PARTY FOOD AT HALLOWEEN TIME. MAKE IT THE CENTERPIECE OF YOUR BUFFET TABLE BY SERVING IT IN A LARGE, HOLLOWED-OUT PUMPKIN OR AN OLD CAST-IRON "CAULDRON."

2 pounds pumpkin or butternut squash, peeled and seeded
1 tablespoon safflower oil
1 large onion, chopped
1 garlic clove, minced
1 jalapeño, minced
2 large tomatoes, chopped
1 cup water
1 cup apple juice
¼ cup tomato paste
4 tablespoons chili powder, commercial or homemade (pages 7-8)
1 teaspoon salt
⅛ teaspoon cayenne
3 cups cooked black beans

Cut pumpkin or squash into ½-inch chunks, and set aside. Heat the oil in a large chili pot over medium heat. Add the onion, garlic, and jalapeño. Cover, and cook, stirring occasionally, until softened, about 5 minutes. Add the reserved pumpkin, tomatoes, water, apple juice, tomato paste, chili powder, salt, and cayenne, and stir well. Bring to a boil, lower the heat, cover, and simmer until the pumpkin is tender, about 30 minutes. Add the black beans, and more water if

Over the Top

Add variety and flair with one or more of the following delicious chili toppings:

- *diced avocado sprinkled with lime juice*
- *sour cream (dairy or non-dairy)*
- *chopped red onions*
- *chopped scallions*
- *hot or mild salsa*
- *chopped marinated artichokes*
- *minced jalapeños*
- *sliced black olives*
- *shredded lettuce*
- *guacamole*
- *grated soy cheese*
- *grated Monterey jack or cheddar cheese*

the chili is too thick for your taste. Cover, and continue to simmer about 15 minutes to blend flavors. Serve with your choice of garnishes or toppings.

SERVES 6

WHITE BEAN THREE-TOMATO CHILI

THIS RECIPE USES FRESH, CANNED, AND SUN-DRIED TOMA-TOES FOR A RICH DEPTH OF FLAVOR. CANNELLINI OR NAVY BEANS ARE OTHER WHITE BEANS THAT MAY BE USED IN PLACE OF GREAT NORTHERN BEANS.

1 tablespoon safflower oil
1 medium onion, chopped
1 red bell pepper, chopped
1 garlic clove, minced
2 large ripe tomatoes, diced
1 can (28-ounce) Italian plum tomatoes, chopped
¾ cup oil-packed sun-dried tomatoes, drained and
    chopped
4 tablespoons mild chili powder (page 8)
2 cups water
3 cups cooked Great Northern beans
Salt and fresh-ground black pepper to taste

Heat the oil in a large chili pot over medium heat. Add the onion, bell pepper, and garlic, cover, and cook until the onion is softened, about 5 minutes. Add the fresh tomatoes, canned tomatoes, sun-dried tomatoes, chili powder, water, beans and salt and pepper, lower the heat, and simmer about 30 minutes.

SERVES 6

CHILI WITH CHAYOTE

🍅 🍅 🍅

CHAYOTE IS A SMALL, LIGHT GREEN PEAR-SHAPED SQUASH, NATIVE TO MEXICO AND CENTRAL AMERICA. ITS DELICATE FLAVOR COMPLEMENTS THE SPICINESS OF THE CHILI SEASONINGS. I LIKE THE DRAMATIC COLOR CONTRAST OF THE PALE GREEN CHAYOTE AND THE DEEP RED KIDNEY BEANS.

1 pound chayote, halved and seeded
1 tablespoon safflower oil
1 large onion, chopped
2 garlic cloves, minced
1 jalapeño, seeded and minced
1 small green bell pepper, chopped
1 can (28-ounce) crushed tomatoes
3 tablespoons chili powder, commercial or homemade
    (pages 7-8)
1 teaspoon ground cumin
2 tablespoons vegetarian Worcestershire sauce
2 cups water
¾ teaspoon salt
⅛ teaspoon fresh-ground black pepper
3 cups cooked dark red kidney beans
Low-fat sour cream or tofu sour cream, as
    accompaniment
Hot or mild salsa, as accompaniment

Cut the chayote into ½-inch cubes, and set aside. Heat the oil in a large chili pot over medium heat. Add the onion, garlic, and jalapeño, cover, and cook until softened, about 5 minutes. Add the chayote and bell pepper, and continue cooking until the vegetables begin to soften, about 10 minutes. Add the tomatoes, chili powder, cumin, Worcestershire sauce, water, and salt and pepper. Bring to a boil, lower the heat, and simmer, uncovered, for 20 minutes. Add the kidney beans, and simmer 15 minutes longer. Serve, accompanied by small bowls of sour cream and salsa to use as toppings.

SERVES 6

CHILI VERDE

THIS "GREEN CHILI" IS A ST. PATRICK'S DAY TRADITION IN OUR HOUSE. I USUALLY SERVE IT OVER GREEN SPINACH ROTINI AND TOP IT WITH GUACAMOLE FOR A TRULY CROSS-CULTURAL CELEBRATION. FRESH TOMATILLOS LOOK LIKE SMALL GREEN TOMATOES IN PAPERY HUSKS. THEY HAVE A SLIGHTLY TART FLAVOR, AND ARE AVAILABLE IN MOST SUPERMARKETS.

1 tablespoon olive oil
1 medium onion, chopped
2 garlic cloves, minced
1 large green bell pepper, chopped
1 pound green tomatoes, chopped
1 pound tomatillos, husked and chopped
1 teaspoon dried oregano, preferably Mexican
¾ teaspoon ground cumin
1 teaspoon sugar
Salt and fresh-ground black pepper to taste
1½ cups water
3 cups cooked Great Northern beans or other white
    beans
2 cans (4-ounce) diced green chiles, drained
¼ cup chopped parsley, for garnish
¼ cup chopped cilantro, for garnish

eat the oil in a large chili pot over medium heat. Add the onion, garlic, bell pepper, and tomatoes. Cover, and cook until the vegetables begin to soften, about 5 minutes. Add the tomatillos, oregano, cumin, sugar, and salt and pepper. Lower the heat, add the water, and simmer, stirring often, until the mixture is thickened and the vegetables are tender, about 25 minutes. Add the beans and chiles, and simmer 10 minutes longer, or until heated through, adding more water if the chili becomes too dry. Garnish your servings with the chopped parsley and cilantro.

SERVES 4 TO 6

VEGGIE CONFETTI CHILI

RIGHTLY COLORED VEGETABLES ADD VISUAL APPEAL AS WELL AS FLAVOR AND TEXTURE TO THIS RECIPE. VARY THE VEGETABLES ACCORDING TO YOUR TASTE, AND SERVE THE CHILI OVER RICE WITH YOUR FAVORITE CONDIMENTS.

1 tablespoon safflower oil
1 cup chopped red onion
2 medium carrots, diced
2 garlic cloves, minced
1 small green bell pepper, diced
1 small red bell pepper, diced
1 small sweet potato, peeled and diced
2 cups fresh or frozen corn kernels
2 cups diced tomatoes, fresh or canned
4 tablespoons hot chili powder (page 7)
1 can (6-ounce) tomato paste
1 teaspoon ground cumin

Crowd Pleasers

When serving chili to a crowd, make it only moderately spicy and then set out condiments so that guests can increase the degree of heat to their taste. For those who prefer a milder chili, serve sour cream, crudités, shredded lettuce, diced avocados, grated cheese, and tortillas. Genuine fire-eaters will want to choose from a selection of diced chiles (fresh or pickled), hot salsa, hot pepper sauce, crushed red pepper flakes, and chopped onions. To please everyone's palate, include a bowl of cool, creamy coleslaw and a basket of warm cornbread.

1 teaspoon salt
2 cups water or vegetable stock
2 cups cooked pinto beans
1 cup cooked Great Northern beans or other white
  beans

Heat the oil in a large chili pot over medium heat. Add the onion, carrots, and garlic. Cover, and cook until softened, about 5 minutes. Add the bell peppers, sweet potato, corn, tomatoes, chili powder, tomato paste, cumin, salt, and water or stock to the chili pot, and stir to combine. Bring to a boil, stirring frequently. Lower the heat, and simmer, covered, for 30 minutes, or until vegetables are tender. Add the pinto beans, and simmer, uncovered, 15 minutes longer to heat through and thicken.

SERVES 6

ROASTED ROOT VEGETABLE CHILI

THE RICH, MELLOW FLAVOR OF ROASTED ROOT VEGETABLES MAKES THIS A PERFECT CHOICE FOR A LATE AUTUMN MEAL, ACCOMPANIED BY WARM, FRESH CORNBREAD. AS WITH ALL VEGETABLES, BE SURE TO THOROUGHLY WASH THE CARROTS, PARSNIPS, AND POTATO. EVEN IF THEY ARE WELL-SCRUBBED, YOU MAY WANT TO PEEL THEM ALSO, UNLESS THEY ARE ORGANIC.

2 tablespoons safflower oil
1 large onion, chopped
2 large carrots, diced
2 parsnips, diced
1 large potato, diced
Salt and fresh-ground black pepper to taste
1 garlic clove, minced
1 jalapeño, minced
1 can (6-ounce) tomato paste
4 tablespoons chili powder, commercial or homemade
   (pages 7-8)
2 cups water
3 cups cooked pinto beans

Preheat the oven to 400°F. Spread 1 tablespoon of the oil in the bottom of a shallow baking pan. Distribute the onion, carrots, parsnips, and potato in the pan, and toss them to coat them with oil. Sprinkle the vegetables with the salt and pepper, and place the pan in the oven. Roast the vegetables until softened and slightly browned, about 30 minutes, turning them over once.

Meanwhile, heat the remaining oil in a large chili pot over medium heat. Add the garlic and jalapeño, and cook until

fragrant, about 3 minutes. Add the tomato paste, chili powder, water, and some salt to taste, and stir well. Bring to a boil, lower the heat, cover, and simmer 20 minutes to blend flavors. When the roasted vegetables are tender, add them to the pot along with the pinto beans, and simmer 15 minutes longer.

SERVES 6

SUN-DRIED TOMATO CHILI

THIS FULL-BODIED CHILI COMBINES MEATY SEITAN CHUNKS WITH A GROUND BEEF ALTERNATIVE FOR GREAT TASTE AND TEXTURE. THE SUN-DRIED TOMATOES ADD A RICH, SMOKY FLAVOR THAT IS ESPECIALLY ENHANCED WHEN THE CHILI IS SERVED OVER PASTA.

2 tablespoons safflower oil
8 ounces seitan (about 2 cups), cubed
1 cup oil-packed sun-dried tomatoes, drained and
    chopped
1 medium onion, minced
2 garlic cloves, minced
¼ cup tomato paste
3 tablespoons chili powder, commercial or homemade
    (pages 7-8)
1 teaspoon dried oregano, preferably Mexican
1 teaspoon salt
2 cups tomato juice
1 package (12-ounce) cooked ground beef alternative
    (page 12)

Heat 1 tablespoon of the oil in a large skillet over medium-high heat. Add the seitan, and cook until browned on all sides, about 5 minutes. Set aside.

Heat the remaining 1 tablespoon oil in a large chili pot over medium heat. Add the sun-dried tomatoes, onion, and garlic, cover, and cook until the onion is softened, about 5 minutes. Add the tomato paste, chili powder, oregano, salt, and tomato juice. Bring to a boil, lower the heat, and simmer 30 minutes. Add the ground beef alternative and the reserved seitan, and additional water if the chili is too thick for your taste. Simmer 15 minutes longer to heat through and blend flavors.

SERVES 4 TO 6

SUCCOTASH CHILI WITH CRISPY ONION SHREDS

CORN AND LIMA BEANS HAVE A NATURAL AFFINITY FOR CHILI SEASONS. THE MILD CHILI POWDER HELPS TO CREATE A TAME YET FLAVORFUL CHILI WHICH CAN DOUBLE AS A VEGETABLE SIDE DISH. THE ONION SHREDS ADD TEXTURE AND FLAVOR, AND CAN BE USED AS A TOPPING ON ANY OF THE CHILI RECIPES AS A NICE CHANGE FROM CHOPPED RAW ONION.

4 cups (2 packages) frozen succotash
3 tablespoons safflower oil
1 large onion, chopped
1 garlic clove, minced
4 tablespoons mild chili powder (page 8)
1 teaspoon dried savory
3 cups diced tomatoes, fresh or canned, drained
1½ cups water
Salt and fresh-ground black pepper to taste
1 large onion, halved lengthwise

Cook the succotash according to package directions, and set aside. Preheat the oven to 325°F.

Heat the oil in a large chili pot over medium heat. Add the chopped onion, and garlic. Cover, and cook until the onion is softened, about 5 minutes. Add the chili powder, savory, tomatoes, water, and salt and pepper. Bring to a boil, lower the heat, and simmer 30 minutes, adding more water if necessary.

Meanwhile, prepare the crispy onion shreds: Using a sharp knife, cut the onion halves into paper-thin half-ring slices. Press the onion slices between several thicknesses of paper towels to remove excess moisture. Separate the onion slices into shreds, and place in a medium bowl. Add the remaining 2 tablespoons oil, and toss to coat. Distribute the onions on a lightly oiled baking pan and bake until browned, about 25 minutes, stirring frequently to ensure even browning. Be careful not to burn the onions. Set the onions aside and cool them to room temperature to allow them to crisp. Add cooked succotash and cook 10 minutes longer to heat through and blend flavors.

Add the cooked succotash to the chili pot, and simmer 10 minutes longer to heat through and blend flavors. Serve, garnished with the crispy onion shreds.

SERVES 4 TO 6

MEDITERRANEAN CHILI WITH RED PEPPER COULIS

SERVE THIS CHILI OVER PASTA ACCOMPANIED BY GARLIC BREAD TO FURTHER COMPLEMENT THE MEDITERRANEAN FLAVORS. THE SULTRY RED PEPPER COULIS GARNISH CAN BE MADE IN SECONDS WITH JARRED ROASTED RED PEPPERS.

1½ tablespoons olive oil
1 large onion, chopped
2 pounds zucchini, chopped coarse
3 garlic cloves, minced fine
1 can (6-ounce) tomato paste
4 tablespoons chili powder, commercial or homemade
(pages 7-8)
1 teaspoon dried oregano
2 cups diced tomatoes, fresh or canned
2 cups water
3 cups cooked chickpeas
½ cup sliced ripe olives
1 tablespoon capers, rinsed and chopped
Salt to taste
1 jar (4-ounce) roasted red peppers

Heat the oil in a large chili pot over medium heat. Add the onion, zucchini, and garlic, cover, and cook until the onion is softened, about 5 minutes. Add the tomato paste, chili powder, oregano, tomatoes, and water. Bring to a boil, lower the heat, and simmer, uncovered, for 20 minutes. Add the chickpeas, olives, capers, and salt. Simmer 15 minutes longer, or until the flavors are well blended, adding more water if necessary.

Meanwhile, drain the roasted red peppers, reserving 1 tablespoon of the oil. Cut the peppers into large pieces, and place in a food processor or blender along with the reserved oil. Purée until smooth, adding salt and pepper to taste. Transfer coulis to a small bowl. To serve, drizzle 1 tablespoon or more of the coulis over each portion of the chili.

SERVES 6

THREE SISTERS CHILI

ACCORDING TO IROQUOIS LEGEND, BEANS, CORN, AND SQUASH ARE THE "THREE SISTERS" BECAUSE THEY WERE ALWAYS PLANTED TOGETHER AND EATEN TOGETHER, LIKE INSEPARABLE SIBLINGS. ONE TASTE OF THIS COLORFUL CHILI AND YOU'LL BE GLAD THEY'RE INSEPARABLE.

1 small butternut squash, peeled, halved, and seeded
1 tablespoon olive oil
1 medium onion, chopped
½ cup chopped celery
2 garlic cloves, minced
1 can (6-ounce) tomato paste
3 tablespoons mild chili powder (page 8)
1 teaspoon dried oregano, preferably Mexican
½ teaspoon dried basil
Salt and fresh-ground black pepper to taste
2 cups diced tomatoes, fresh or canned
2 cups tomato juice
2 cups fresh or frozen corn kernels
3 cups cooked pinto beans

Cut the squash into ½-inch thick chunks. Heat the oil in a large chili pot over medium heat. Add the squash, onion, celery, and garlic. Cover, and cook until the vegetables begin to soften, about 10 minutes. Stir in the tomato paste, chili powder, oregano, basil, and salt and pepper. Add the tomatoes and tomato juice. Bring to a boil, lower the heat, and simmer, covered, until the vegetables are tender, about 20 minutes. Add the corn and pinto beans, and simmer 20 minutes longer, uncovered, to thicken and blend flavors. Taste, and correct seasonings. Serve with your favorite accompaniments.

SERVES 6

JUNE'S MIDNIGHT MOON CHILI

Y FRIEND JUNE ROBBINS MAKES THIS CHUNKY VEGETABLE CHILI BY THE LIGHT OF THE MOON, SINCE HER BUSY SCHEDULE DICTATES THAT SHE DO HER COOKING LATE IN THE EVENING. A LATE-NIGHT PREPARATION GIVES THE FLAVORS TIME TO BLEND BEFORE SERVING THE CHILI THE NEXT DAY.

1½ tablespoons olive oil
3 large garlic cloves, chopped
1 can (28-ounce) whole peeled tomatoes, drained and diced
1 can (28-ounce) crushed tomatoes
1 small jalapeño, minced
1 can (15-ounce) dark red kidney beans
2 cans (15-ounce) light red kidney beans
4 tablespoons chili powder, commercial or homemade (pages 7-8)
2 teaspoons ground cumin
1 teaspoon salt
1 tablespoon chopped fresh cilantro
1 cup water
1 large onion, cut into 8 wedges
2 celery ribs, cut into 2-inch chunks
1 green bell pepper, cut into 2-inch dice
1 red bell pepper, cut into 2-inch dice
1 yellow bell pepper, cut into 2-inch dice
2 cups frozen corn kernels
Tofu sour cream, as accompaniment

eat the oil in a large chili pot over medium heat. Add the garlic, and cook until it becomes fragrant, about 1 minute. Add the tomatoes, jalapeño, kidney beans, chili powder,

All-in-One Condiment Bowl

Instead of setting out individual bowls of condiments, consider combining your favorites to make a unique, fresh-tasting topping that blends several chili-enhancing flavors. Simply combine all the following ingredients in a small bowl, cover, and chill. Place the condiment bowl on the table when the chili is served.

1 avocado, diced

1 fresh ripe tomato, diced

1 small red onion, chopped

3 tablespoons fresh lime juice

1 tablespoon olive oil

½ teaspoon sugar

½ teaspoon salt

cumin, salt, cilantro, and water. Bring to a boil, lower the heat, and add the onion, celery, bell peppers, and corn. Simmer, covered, until the vegetables are tender, about 30 minutes. Remove cover, and simmer 15 minutes longer, or until desired consistency is reached. Top each serving with a dollop of tofu sour cream.

SERVES 6

TWO-POTATO CHILI

THE SUBTLY SWEET FLAVORS OF TWO KINDS OF POTATOES ARE COMPLEMENTED BY THE SPICINESS OF THE CHILI SEASONINGS HERE. IF YOU CAN'T FIND FRESH MILD CHILES, USE CANNED ONES.

1 tablespoon safflower oil

1 large onion, chopped

1 garlic clove, chopped

4 tablespoons chili powder, commercial or homemade (pages 7-8)

3 mild green chiles, seeded and chopped

1 can (28-ounce) crushed tomatoes

¼ cup tomato paste

2 large white potatoes, peeled and diced

2 large sweet potatoes, peeled and diced

1 teaspoon salt

2½ cups water

2 cups cooked pinto beans

1 teaspoon cumin (optional)

Heat the oil in a large chili pot over medium heat. Add the onion and garlic, cover, and cook until softened, about 5 minutes. Stir in the chili powder, chiles, tomatoes, tomato paste, potatoes, salt, and water. Bring to a boil, lower the heat, and simmer, covered, until the vegetables are tender, about 30 minutes. Add the pinto beans and, if you wish, cumin, and simmer 10 minutes longer. Taste, and adjust seasonings. For a thicker chili, purée 2 cups of the mixture in a blender and stir it back in to the pot.

SERVES 6

SPICY FAVA BEAN CHILI

FAVAS ARE LARGE, MEATY BEANS THAT RESEMBLE LIMAS. THEY ARE WELL KNOWN IN EUROPE AND ARE GAINING POPULARITY IN THE UNITED STATES. FOR A MILDER VERSION OF THIS RECIPE, OMIT THE SERRANO CHILE. I LIKE TO SERVE THIS CHILI OVER FRESH-COOKED MILLET, TOPPED WITH CHOPPED, MARINATED ARTI-CHOKE HEARTS.

1 tablespoon olive oil
2 Anaheim chiles, chopped
1 serrano chile, seeded, and minced
2 cups chopped onions
3 garlic cloves, minced
4 tablespoons chili powder, commercial or homemade
   (pages 7-8)
1 teaspoon ground cumin
1 teaspoon dried oregano, preferably Mexican
1 teaspoon paprika

1 cup oil-packed sun-dried tomatoes, drained and
   chopped
1 cup tomato purée
1 cup water
3 cups cooked fava beans
1 teaspoon salt
⅛ teaspoon fresh-ground black pepper
1 jar (4-ounce) marinated artichoke hearts, drained
   and chopped, for garnish

Heat the oil in a large chili pot over medium heat. Add the chiles, onions, and garlic, cover, and cook until softened, about 5 minutes. Stir in the chili powder, cumin, oregano, and paprika. Add the tomatoes, purée, water, fava beans, salt, and pepper. Bring to a boil, lower the heat, and simmer, covered, until the vegetables are tender, about 30 minutes. Taste, and adjust seasonings. Simmer, uncovered, 10 minutes longer, or until desired consistency is reached. Serve the chili garnished with the chopped marinated artichoke hearts.

SERVES 4

EGGPLANT AND PORTOBELLO MUSHROOM CHILI

THE EGGPLANT AND THE PORTOBELLO MUSHROOMS ADD A CHEWY, MEATY TEXTURE TO THIS FRESH-TASTING CHILI. IT'S DELICIOUS SERVED OVER PASTA OR POLENTA.

1 eggplant, peeled and cut into ½-inch dice
1 tablespoon salt
1 tablespoon olive oil
1 large onion, chopped
1 red bell pepper, diced
4 large portobello mushrooms, chopped
3 garlic cloves, minced
8 fresh plum tomatoes, diced
3 tablespoons chili powder,commercial or homemade
   (pages 7-8)
1 teaspoon dried oregano, preferably Mexican
1 cup tomato juice
1 cup water
Salt and fresh-ground black pepper to taste
2 tablespoons chopped fresh parsley,
   for garnish
2 tablespoons chopped fresh basil, for garnish

Place the diced eggplant in a strainer, toss it with the salt, and let it stand for 1 hour to remove excess moisture. Pat eggplant dry with paper towels.

Heat the oil in a large chili pot over medium heat. Add the onion, bell pepper, mushrooms, garlic, and reserved eggplant. Cover, and cook until the vegetables have softened, about 10 minutes. Add the tomatoes, chili powder, oregano, tomato juice, water, and salt and pepper. Lower the heat,

and simmer 30 minutes, stirring occasionally. Taste, and adjust seasonings. Garnish with fresh parsley and basil.

SERVES 6

BLACK BEAN CHILI WITH CILANTRO PESTO

THE CILANTRO PESTO ADDS A FRAGRANT TOUCH TO THIS CHILI, BUT IT'S FLAVORFUL ENOUGH TO STAND ON ITS OWN, IF YOU PREFER TO OMIT THE PESTO.

1 tablespoon olive oil
1 large onion, chopped
½ cup chopped celery
2 garlic cloves, minced
1 can (6-ounce) tomato paste
1 can (16-ounce) whole tomatoes, chopped
3 tablespoons chili powder
1 teaspoon ground cumin
2 cups water
Salt and fresh-ground black pepper to taste
2 tablespoons lemon juice
4 cups cooked black beans
½ cup Cilantro Pesto (recipe follows)

Heat the oil in a large chili pot over medium heat. Add the onion, celery, and garlic, cover, and cook until softened, about 5 minutes. Add the tomato paste, tomatoes, chili powder, cumin, water, and salt and pepper. Lower the heat, and simmer 30 minutes. Add the lemon juice, black beans, and more water

if needed. Simmer 15 minutes longer, or until desired consistency is reached. Just before serving, swirl in the cilantro pesto.

SERVES 6

CILANTRO PESTO

1 cup packed fresh cilantro leaves
½ cup almonds
3 large garlic cloves
¼ cup grated parmesan (or soy parmesan)
¼ cup olive oil
½ teaspoon salt

Combine the cilantro, almonds, and garlic in a food processor and purée until smooth. Add the parmesan, oil, and salt, and purée to a smooth paste.

MAKES ABOUT 1 CUP

DESERT CACTUS CHILI

NAPOLITOS, OR NOPALES, ARE THE LEAVES OF THE PRICKLY PEAR CACTUS. THEY ARE AVAILABLE CANNED OR IN JARS IN SPECIALTY FOOD STORES OR IN THE MEXICAN FOODS SECTION OF MOST SUPERMARKETS.

2½ cups textured soy protein granules
2 tablespoons olive oil
1 medium onion, chopped
2 garlic cloves, minced
4 tablespoons chili powder, commercial or homemade (pages 7-8)
2 Anaheim chiles, seeded and chopped fine
3 large green tomatoes, chopped
1½ cups tomato purée
1½ cups water
3 tomatillos, husked and chopped
1 jar (8-ounce) nopalitos, rinsed, drained, and chopped
Salt and fresh-ground black pepper to taste

Rehydrate the soy granules in water according to package directions, and set aside. Heat the oil in a large chili pot over medium heat. Add the onion and garlic, cover, and cook until softened, about 5 minutes. Add the chili powder, chiles, green tomatoes, tomato purée, reserved soy granules, and water. Bring to a boil, lower the heat, and simmer, covered, for 30 minutes. Add the tomatillos, nopalitos, and salt and pepper, and simmer 15 minutes longer to heat through and blend flavors.

SERVES 6

ALTERED STATES

INCLUDED IN THIS CHAPTER ARE MEATLESS INTERPRETATIONS OF CLASSIC REGIONAL CHILI RECIPES FROM ALL OVER THE UNITED STATES, INCLUDING NEW MEXICO, CINCINNATI, AND, OF COURSE, TEXAS. SINCE I'M AMONG THOSE WHO BELIEVE THAT CHILI IS A STATE OF MIND, I CROSSED INTERNATIONAL BORDERS TO COME UP WITH GLOBALLY INSPIRED CREATIONS. THESE DISHES USE A VARIETY OF GRAINS, BEANS, VEGETABLES, AND SEASONINGS. WITH INGREDIENTS LIKE THE FRAGRANT JERK SEASONINGS OF JAMAICA AND THE INTOXICATING SPICES OF INDIAN CURRY, THESE RECIPES HELP TO PROVE THAT CHILI CAN BE A UNIVERSAL PLEASURE.

SOUTHWESTERN CHILI REVISITED

IN THE TRADITIONAL SOUTHWESTERN STYLE, THE BEANS AND THE CHILI ARE SERVED SEPARATELY HERE, RATHER THAN COMBINED IN ONE POT. NOTICE THE ABSENCE OF TOMATOES AND MOST OTHER VEGETABLES FROM THIS CLASSIC INTERPRETATION. I ESPECIALLY LIKE THE CHEWY TEXTURE OF THE TEXTURED SOY PROTEIN CHUNKS, ALTHOUGH CUBED SEITAN OR TEMPEH ALSO WORK WELL AND MAY BE SUBSTITUTED. A PRE-BLENDED CHILI POWDER CAN BE USED INSTEAD OF THE GROUND CHILES IN THIS RECIPE.

2½ cups textured soy protein chunks
1 tablespoon safflower oil
1 medium onion, chopped
2 garlic cloves, minced
3 tablespoons ground red chiles
1 teaspoon dried oregano, preferably Mexican
1 teaspoon ground cumin
1 teaspoon salt
⅛ teaspoon fresh-ground black pepper
3 cups water or vegetable stock
4 cups cooked pinto beans

Reconstitute the soy chunks in water according to package directions, and set aside. Heat the oil in a large chili pot over medium heat. Add the onion and garlic, cover, and cook until the onion is softened, about 5 minutes. Add the ground chiles, oregano, cumin, salt, and pepper. Stir in the water, and add the reserved soy chunks. Cook, uncovered, for 1 hour, or until desired consistency is reached. Just before serving, heat the cooked pinto beans in a separate saucepan.

To serve, divide beans evenly among bowls and top with the chili, or serve the chili separately, according to individual preference.

SERVES 6

ANASAZI CHILI WITH QUINOA

🍅 🍅 🍅

THE ANASAZI IS A SWEET, MEATY BEAN, WHOSE NAME MEANS "THE ANCIENT ONES" IN THE NAVAJO LANGUAGE. PAIRED WITH FRESH-COOKED QUINOA, THE HIGH-PROTEIN GRAIN OF THE ANCIENT INCAS, IT BECOMES A DISH STEEPED IN NATIVE AMERICAN HERITAGE. IF ANASAZI BEANS ARE UNAVAILABLE, USE PINTO OR KIDNEY BEANS.

1 tablespoon safflower oil
1 large onion, chopped fine
1 red bell pepper, chopped
3 tablespoons chili powder, commercial or homemade
    (pages 7-8)
1 teaspoon ground cumin
1 teaspoon dried oregano, preferably Mexican
1 teaspoon salt
⅛ teaspoon fresh-ground black pepper
4 cups chopped plum tomatoes, fresh or canned
3 cups cooked anasazi beans
1½ cups water

Heat the oil in a large chili pot over medium heat. Add the onion and bell pepper, cover, and cook until the onion is softened, about 5 minutes. Add the chili powder, cumin, oregano, salt, and pepper. Stir to blend. Add the tomatoes, anasazi beans, and water. Bring to a boil, lower the heat, and

Through Thick and Thin

🍅

Should chili be thin and soupy, or thick and substantial? Many opt for somewhere in between. Here are some tips to get you through the thick and thin of chili making:

For thick chili:
• cook with the pot uncovered
• purée a cup or two of the chili and stir back into the pot
• near the end of cooking time, stir in about 2 tablespoons masa harina (corn flour) mixed with enough cold water to make a paste
• use less liquid to begin with

For thin chili:
• add more water or other liquid
• keep the pot covered during cooking

simmer 30 minutes, stirring occasionally. Taste, and adjust seasonings. Spoon the chili over hot quinoa.

SERVES 4

TEX-MEX TEMPEH CHILI

N O, TEMPEH IS NOT A CITY IN ARIZONA — IT'S COMPRESSED SOYBEANS FORMED INTO CAKES. TEMPEH'S MEAT-LIKE TEX-TURE AND HIGH PROTEIN CONTENT MAKE IT A NATURAL INGREDI-ENT FOR VEGETARIAN CHILI.

2 tablespoons olive oil
1 pound tempeh, diced
1 cup chopped onion
2 garlic cloves, minced
2 jalapeños, stemmed, seeded, and minced
4 tablespoons hot chili powder (page 7)
1 teaspoon ground cumin
1 teaspoon dried oregano, preferably Mexican
1 can (16-ounce) tomato sauce
1 cup water or vegetable stock
Salt and fresh-ground black pepper, to taste

H eat the oil in a large chili pot over medium heat. Add the tempeh and onion, and cook, stirring frequently, until the tempeh is browned and the onion has softened, about 10 min-utes. Add the garlic, jalapeños, chili powder, cumin, oregano, tomato sauce, water, and salt and pepper. Bring to a boil, lower the heat, and simmer 30 minutes, stirring occasionally. Taste, and adjust seasonings, cooking longer, if necessary, until desired consistency is reached.

SERVES 4

FIVE-WAY CINCINNATI CHILI

CHILI IS SERVED IN THIS MANNER THROUGHOUT CINCINNATI: "2-WAY" IS SERVED OVER SPAGHETTI, "3-WAY" ADDS CHEESE, AND "4-WAY" ADDS CHOPPED ONION TO THE CHEESE. TO MAKE 5-WAY CHILI, START WITH A LAYER OF COOKED BEANS. FOR AN AUTHENTIC FINISH, GARNISH WITH CRUMBLED OYSTER CRACKERS.

2½ pounds textured soy protein granules
2 tablespoons olive oil
1 large onion, chopped
2 garlic cloves, minced
3 tablespoons mild chili powder (page 8)
1 teaspoon cinnamon
1 teaspoon paprika
1 teaspoon allspice
2 cups tomato sauce
1 cup water
2 tablespoons red wine vinegar
2 tablespoons light brown sugar
1 pound cooked spaghetti
2 cups cooked kidney beans
1 cup grated cheddar or soy cheese, for garnish
1 cup chopped red onion, for garnish

Rehydrate the soy granules in water according to package directions, and set aside. Heat water in a large pot for the spaghetti.

Heat the oil in a large chili pot over medium heat. Add the onion and garlic, cover, and cook until softened, about 5 minutes. Add the chili powder, cinnamon, paprika, and allspice, and stir to coat the onion. Add the tomato sauce, water, vinegar, and brown sugar, lower the heat, and simmer 20 minutes. Add the reserved soy granules, and simmer 15

minutes longer, or until desired consistency is reached.

Meanwhile, cook the spaghetti until *al dente*, and drain. Just prior to serving, heat the kidney beans. Spoon a layer of beans in the bottom of each bowl. Top with a layer of spaghetti, then a ladleful of chili, then grated cheese and chopped onion as a garnish.

SERVES 4

LOUISIANA BAYOU CHILI

FILÉ POWDER, WHICH IS MADE FROM GROUND SASSAFRAS LEAVES, IS AN INGREDIENT FOUND IN GUMBOS AND OTHER CREOLE DISHES. IT IS AVAILABLE IN MOST SUPERMARKETS AND SPECIALTY FOOD SHOPS. SERVE THIS CHILI OVER RICE, WITH A BOTTLE OF HOT SAUCE OUT ON THE TABLE FOR THOSE WHO LIKE A LITTLE EXTRA KICK.

1 tablespoon safflower oil
1 cup chopped scallions
2 garlic cloves, minced
3 tablespoons chili powder, commercial or homemade (pages 7-8)
1 teaspoon dried thyme
1 teaspoon filé powder
2 cups diced tomatoes, fresh or canned
1 can (4-ounce) diced green chiles
1 package (12-ounce) cooked ground beef alternative (page 12)
1 cup water
1 teaspoon Louisiana hot sauce
⅛ teaspoon cayenne
Salt and fresh-ground black pepper to taste
3 cups cooked red beans

Heat the oil in a large chili pot over medium heat. Add the scallions and garlic, and cook until the garlic is fragrant, about 2 minutes. Stir in the chili powder, thyme, and filé powder. Add the tomatoes, chiles, ground beef alternative, and water. Bring to a boil, lower the heat, and simmer 10 minutes. Add the hot sauce, cayenne, salt and pepper, and red beans, and simmer 20 minutes longer to blend flavors, stirring occasionally. Taste, and adjust seasonings.

SERVES 6

TEXAS CHILI CON "CARNE" WITH SALSA CREAM

🍅 🍅 🍅

THE "CARNE" IS THE WHEAT-MEAT, OR SEITAN, IN THIS RECIPE FOR "CHILES WITH MEAT." NOTICE THERE ARE NO TOMATOES OR OTHER VEGETABLES — JUST A HINT OF GARLIC IN THIS TRADITIONAL TEXAS-STYLE CHILI. IF SEITAN IS UNAVAILABLE, TEXTURED SOY PROTEIN CHUNKS OR TEMPEH WILL DO.

🍅

1 cup hot or mild salsa
½ cup sour cream or yogurt (dairy or non-dairy)
1 tablespoon safflower oil
1½ pounds seitan, chopped coarse
2 garlic cloves, minced
3 tablespoons hot chili powder (page 7)
1 dried red chile, crushed
1½ teaspoons ground cumin
1 teaspoon paprika
1½ cups water
1 teaspoon salt

The Silence of the Beans

🍅

Some people tend to avoid beans because the complex sugars they contain can cause intestinal gas. However, there are some things you can do if fear of flatulence prevents you from enjoying delicious and nourishing bean dishes.

1. When preparing dried beans, always soak them for a minimum of 4 hours, and then drain the soaking liquid. This will eliminate much of the complex sugars, which are the source of the problem. Cook them in fresh water. (See the chart of bean cooking times on page 10.)

2. Add a 4-inch strip of kombu seaweed to the cooking water. It will aid in diges-

tion, quicken the cooking process, and add nutrients.

3. Use Beano or a similar enzyme product to aid in the digestion of the complex sugars present in beans.

4. Start slow. Eat a small portion of beans at first to get your body used to digesting the complex sugars. Eat more beans over the ensuing weeks. Once your body gets used to eating beans, you can gradually increase the quantities, and your body will adjust.

5. Eat vegetarian chili. Chili made without meat is easier to digest because your stomach doesn't have to work as hard.

6. If you are using canned beans, drain and rinse them well. Use a good quality organic canned bean such as the Eden brand.

Combine the salsa and sour cream or yogurt in a food processor and purée until well blended. Transfer to a small bowl, cover, and refrigerate.

Heat the oil in a large chili pot over medium heat. Add the seitan, and cook until browned, about 5 minutes. Stir in the garlic, chili powder, chile, cumin, and paprika. Add the water and salt. Bring to a boil, lower the heat, and simmer 30 minutes, to blend flavors. Taste, and adjust seasonings, adding more water if necessary. Serve the chili with a dollop of salsa cream on each serving.

SERVES 6

WEST COAST CHILI

CALIFORNIA OLIVES AND AVOCADOS COMBINED WITH THE VIBRANT COLORS OF FRESH VEGETABLES CONTRIBUTE TO THE WEST COAST MOOD OF THIS CHILI. TO COMPLETE THE PICTURE, SERVE WITH A BOTTLE OF GOOD CALIFORNIA WINE AND SOME SAN FRANCISCO SOURDOUGH BREAD.

1 tablespoon olive oil
1 medium onion, chopped
1 red bell pepper, chopped
1 yellow bell pepper, chopped
1 garlic clove, minced
8 fresh plum tomatoes, diced
¼ cup tomato paste
3 tablespoons chili powder, commercial or homemade
   (pages 7-8)
½ teaspoon dried oregano, preferably Mexican
Salt to taste
1 cup dry red wine
½ cup water
3 cups cooked kidney beans
2 avocados, diced, for garnish
½ cup sliced pitted ripe olives, for garnish
½ cup grated Monterey jack or soy cheese, for garnish

Heat the oil in a large chili pot over medium heat. Add the onion, bell peppers, and garlic, and cook until the vegetables are softened, about 10 minutes. Add the tomatoes, tomato paste, chili powder, oregano, salt, red wine, water, and kidney beans. Bring to a boil, lower the heat, and simmer, covered, for 30 minutes, or until flavors are blended and desired consistency is reached, adding additional water if the

mixture becomes too dry. Serve the chili garnished with the diced avocado, sliced olives, and grated cheese.

SERVES 6

STRICTLY SOUTHERN CHILI

THIS CHILI HAS AN UNUSUAL TWIST BY FEATURING TRADITION-ALLY SOUTHERN INGREDIENTS: COLLARD GREENS AND BLACK-EYED PEAS. HAVING LIVED FOR MANY YEARS IN THE BEAUTIFUL CITY OF CHARLESTON, SOUTH CAROLINA, I CREATED THIS RECIPE AS AN HOMAGE TO THE SOUTH. IF COLLARD GREENS ARE UNAVAIL-ABLE, SUBSTITUTE ANOTHER DARK, LEAFY GREEN, SUCH AS KALE. SERVE THE CHILI OVER HOT RICE WITH A DOLLOP OF SOUR CREAM ON EACH SERVING.

1 tablespoon canola oil
2 medium onions, chopped
2 medium carrots, diced
2 cups chopped collard greens
1 garlic clove, minced
3 tablespoons chili powder, commercial or homemade
  (pages 7-8)
3 cups diced tomatoes, fresh or canned
1½ cups water
1 teaspoon salt
1 teaspoon Louisiana hot sauce
3 cups cooked black-eyed peas

Heat the oil in a large pot over medium heat. Add the onions and carrots, cover, and cook until the onion is softened, about 5 minutes. Add the collard greens and garlic, and cook, covered, 5 minutes longer to wilt collards. Add the chili powder, tomatoes, water, salt, and hot sauce. Bring to a boil, lower the heat, and simmer 30 minutes, or until the vegetables are tender. Add the black-eyed peas, and simmer 10 minutes longer to blend flavors, adding more water if necessary. Taste, and adjust seasonings.

SERVES 6

WORLD'S FAIR CHILI

CHILI WAS INTRODUCED TO THE REST OF THE WORLD AT THE 1904 ST. LOUIS WORLD'S FAIR. THIS MIDWESTERN-STYLE CHILI, WITH ITS SUBTLE SWEETNESS AND ABSENCE OF GARLIC, IS DELICIOUS EVEN WHEN THE WORLD SEEMS *UN*FAIR.

1 pound tempeh
1 tablespoon safflower oil
2 medium onions, chopped fine
2 cups diced tomatoes, fresh or canned
1 can (4-ounce) diced green chiles
3 tablespoons chili powder, commercial or homemade
   (pages 7-8)
1 tablespoon brown sugar
1 tablespoon cider vinegar
1 teaspoon dried oregano, preferably Mexican
1 teaspoon salt
1 cup tomato juice
1 cup water
3 cups cooked kidney beans

Crumble the tempeh, and cook it in the oil in a large chili pot over medium heat, until lightly browned. Add the onions, cover, and cook until softened, about 5 minutes. Stir in the tomatoes, chiles, chili powder, brown sugar, vinegar, oregano, and salt. Add the tomato juice and water, and bring

Go-Togethers

Chili does not have to stand alone. Here are some ways to enjoy it:

- *coleslaw*
- *corn chips*
- *tostadas or soft tortillas*
- *oyster crackers*
- *saltines*
- *cornbread, corn muffins, or corn sticks*
- *crudités: sliced celery, carrots, cucumbers, and other raw veggies*
- *in a pita*
- *over:*
   rice
   pasta
   polenta
   couscous

to a boil. Lower the heat, add the kidney beans, and simmer 30 minutes.

SERVES 4 TO 6

JAMAICAN JERK CHILI

THE HEADY INTENSITY OF JAMAICAN JERK SPICES ARE READILY ABSORBED BY THE TEMPEH, MAKING THIS CHILI ESPECIALLY FLAVORFUL. TRY TO USE TAMARI SAUCE RATHER THAN SOY SAUCE: IT IS OF HIGHER QUALITY AND HAS A BETTER FLAVOR, AND IT IS AVAILABLE IN THE INTERNATIONAL SECTION OF MANY SUPER-MARKETS. TRY THIS CHILI SERVED OVER RICE, WITH CHUTNEY AND CHOPPED PEANUTS AS ACCOMPANIMENTS.

3 tablespoons ground chiles
1 teaspoon ground cinnamon
1 teaspoon ground allspice
1 teaspoon dried oregano, preferably Mexican
1 teaspoon ground cumin
1 teaspoon brown sugar
½ teaspoon cayenne
¼ teaspoon ground nutmeg
¼ teaspoon ground coriander
1 pound tempeh, crumbled
2 tablespoons oil
3 garlic cloves
1 medium onion, minced
8 fresh plum tomatoes, chopped
1 cup water
1 tablespoon rum
1 tablespoon tamari sauce
Salt to taste

In a small bowl, combine the chiles, cinnamon, allspice, oregano, cumin, brown sugar, cayenne, nutmeg, and coriander. Add the tempeh, and toss to coat. Heat 1 tablespoon of the oil in a large skillet over medium heat, and add the tempeh pieces (reserving any remaining spice mixture) and cook until lightly browned, about 5 minutes. Set aside.

Heat the remaining 1 tablespoon oil in a large chili pot over medium heat. Add the garlic and onion, cover, and cook until softened, about 5 minutes. Add the reserved tempeh and tomatoes, and stir to combine. Add the reserved spice mixture along with the water, rum, and tamari. Bring to a boil, lower the heat, add the salt, and simmer until the flavors are blended, about 30 minutes. Serve over rice.

SERVES 4

MOROCCAN-INSPIRED CHILI WITH COUSCOUS

THE APPLE JUICE AND ALLSPICE ADD A SPICY SWEETNESS TO THIS EXOTIC-TASTING CHILI. COUSCOUS CAN BE READY IN MINUTES, SO IF YOU'VE MADE YOUR CHILI IN ADVANCE, THIS CAN TRULY BE A "FAST-FOOD" MEAL.

1 tablespoon olive oil
1 medium onion, chopped
1 jalapeño, minced
3 garlic cloves, minced
3 tablespoons mild chili powder (page 8)
1 teaspoon dried marjoram
½ teaspoon allspice

4 cups diced plum tomatoes, fresh or canned
2 cups apple juice
3 cups cooked chickpeas
1 package (12-ounce) cooked ground beef alternative
  (page 12)
1 cup frozen green peas, thawed
Salt to taste
2 tablespoons minced scallions, for garnish

Heat the oil in a large chili pot over medium heat. Add the onion, jalapeño, and garlic, cover, and cook until softened, about 5 minutes. Add the chili powder, marjoram, and allspice. Stir in the tomatoes and apple juice. Lower the heat, and simmer, covered, for 20 minutes, stirring occasionally. Add the chickpeas, ground beef alternative, peas, and salt, and simmer 10 minutes longer, or until desired consistency is reached. Serve over couscous, and garnish with the minced scallions.

SERVES 6

BOMBAY CHILI WITH CHUTNEY

SERVE THIS FRAGRANT, INDIAN-STYLE CHILI OVER BASMATI RICE ACCOMPANIED BY SMALL BOWLS OF CURRY GARNISHES, SUCH AS YOGURT OR SOUR CREAM, MINCED SCALLIONS, CHOPPED PEANUTS, AND CHUTNEY. IT IS INTERESTING TO NOTE THAT CHILES, KIDNEY BEANS, AND CUMIN—ALL CLASSIC CHILI INGREDIENTS— ARE FREQUENTLY USED IN INDIAN COOKING.

2 tablespoons olive oil
1 large onion, chopped
2 garlic cloves, minced
1 red bell pepper, diced
1 jalapeño, minced
1 tablespoon ground red chiles
1 tablespoon curry powder
1 teaspoon cumin
½ teaspoon ground coriander
1 can (6-ounce) tomato paste
4 fresh tomatoes, chopped
1 teaspoon salt
1½ cups water
4 cups cooked red kidney beans
½ cup spicy sweet chutney

Heat the oil in a large chili pot over medium heat. Add the onion, garlic, bell pepper, and jalapeño, cover, and cook until softened, about 5 minutes. Stir in the ground chiles, curry powder, cumin, coriander, and tomato paste. Add the tomatoes, salt, and water. Bring to a boil, lower the heat, and simmer 30 minutes. Stir in the kidney beans and chutney, and

Chili Spices

Whether blended into chili powder or added separately, cumin and oregano are staples of nearly all chili recipes. Cumin, a member of the parsley family, has been cultivated since ancient times. Cumin seeds are intensely aromatic, hot, and bitter, and are an essential ingredient in chili powder. Cumin seeds can be purchased whole or already ground. Many people choose to roast cumin seeds before using to bring out their flavor. Oregano, or wild marjoram, is an aromatic herb typically used in Mediterranean cooking. Since Mexican oregano is more pungent and flavorful than the European variety, it is often used to make chili.

simmer 10 minutes longer, or until desired consistency is reached.

SERVES 6

PAN-ASIAN CHILI

THE USE OF ADZUKI BEANS, BOK CHOY, GINGER, TAMARI, AND CHILI PASTE IMBUE THIS CHILI WITH ASIAN CHARACTERISTICS. CILANTRO, A PUNGENT HERB ALSO KNOWN AS CHINESE PARSLEY, IS COMMON TO BOTH ASIAN AND SOUTHWESTERN COOKING. TO COMPLEMENT THE CHILI, SERVE WITH A JAPANESE BEER SUCH AS KIRIN OR SAPPORO.

1 tablespoon safflower oil
1 cup chopped scallions
2 garlic cloves, minced
1 tablespoon minced fresh ginger
1 tablespoon Asian chili paste
2 tablespoons chili powder, commercial or homemade
   (pages 7-8)
1 teaspoon sugar
2 cups fine-chopped bok choy
2 cups diced tomatoes, fresh or canned
2 tablespoons tamari sauce
3 cups cooked adzuki beans
1½ cups water
2 tablespoons minced cilantro, for garnish
1 tablespoon sesame seeds, for garnish

Heat the oil in a large chili pot over medium heat. Add the scallions, garlic, and ginger, and cook until fragrant, about

1 minute. Add the chili paste, chili powder, and sugar, and stir for 2 minutes to develop the flavor. Add the bok choy, and stir until wilted. Add the tomatoes, tamari, adzuki beans, and water. Bring to a boil, lower the heat, and simmer 30 minutes, or until desired consistency is reached. Taste, and adjust seasonings, adding more water if mixture becomes too dry. Serve over rice, and garnish with the minced cilantro and sesame seeds.

SERVES 4

SWEET AND SPICY CHILI

RAISINS, CINNAMON, AND SLIVERED ALMONDS GIVE THIS CHILI A MIDDLE EASTERN, ALMOST INDIAN, QUALITY. YOU MIGHT TRY AN AROMATIC RICE SUCH AS JASMINE OR BASMATI TO COMPLEMENT THE HINT OF SWEETNESS IN THE CHILI.

2½ cups textured soy protein granules
1 tablespoon olive oil
1 cup chopped onion
2 garlic cloves, minced
4 tablespoons chili powder, commercial or homemade
   (pages 7-8)
2 teaspoons light brown sugar
1 teaspoon ground cumin
1 teaspoon cinnamon
1 teaspoon salt
⅛ teaspoon cayenne
3 cups diced tomatoes, fresh or canned
1 can (6-ounce) tomato paste
2 cups apple juice

1 can (4-ounce) diced green chiles
¼ cup seedless raisins
3 cups cooked kidney beans
¼ cup toasted slivered almonds, for garnish

Rehydrate the soy granules in water according to package directions, and set aside. Heat the oil in a large chili pot over medium heat. Add the onion and garlic, cover, and cook until softened, about 5 minutes. Stir in the chili powder, brown sugar, cumin, cinnamon, salt, and cayenne. Add the tomatoes, tomato paste, apple juice, chiles, raisins, kidney beans, and the reserved soy granules. Bring to a boil, lower the heat, and simmer 30 minutes. Taste, and adjust seasonings. Serve the chili over rice, garnished with the slivered almonds.

SERVES 6

ITALIAN CHILI WITH OLIVADA

OLIVADA, A PUREE OF RIPE OLIVES, ADDS RICHNESS TO THIS ZESTY, ITALIAN-STYLE CHILI. POLENTA WOULD MAKE A PERFECT ACCOMPANIMENT, OR YOU CAN SERVE IT OVER YOUR FAVORITE PASTA.

¾ cup ripe olives, pitted
¼ cup olive oil
1 medium onion, chopped
1 fennel bulb, diced
3 garlic cloves, minced
1 small green bell pepper, chopped
2 cups diced tomatoes, fresh or canned
1 can (6-ounce) tomato paste
3 tablespoons chili powder, commercial or homemade
*   (pages 7-8)*
1 tablespoon paprika
1 teaspoon dried oregano
2 cups water
1 teaspoon salt
¼ teaspoon fresh-ground black pepper
½ teaspoon crushed red pepper flakes
2 cups cooked chickpeas
3 cups cooked vegetarian sausage, crumbled

Place the olives in a food processor, and puree. Slowly stream in 3 tablespoons of the oil until well blended. Transfer the olivada to a small bowl, and set aside.

Heat the remaining 1 tablespoon oil in a large chili pot over medium heat. Add the onion, fennel, garlic, and bell pepper, cover, and cook until the vegetables are softened,

about 10 minutes. Add the tomatoes, tomato paste, chili powder, paprika, oregano, water, salt, pepper, red pepper flakes, chickpeas, and vegetarian sausage. Stir well to combine, lower the heat, and simmer, uncovered, for 30 minutes. Serve the chili over polenta or pasta, and drizzle the olivada over each portion.

SERVES 6

ALL FIRED UP

IF YOU'RE LOOKING FOR HOT AND SPICY CHILI, YOU'VE COME TO THE RIGHT PLACE. THE RECIPES IN THIS CHAPTER ARE NOT FOR THE TIMID — THEY FEATURE THE MANY VARIETIES OF FIERY CAPSICUMS.

MANY OF THE RECIPES HERE GET THEIR HEAT AS WELL AS THEIR FLAVOR FROM MORE THAN ONE SOURCE: FRESH CHILES, DRIED CHILES, HOT SALSA, CAYENNE, OR HOT SAUCE. OF COURSE, THEY CAN BE TONED DOWN OR "FIRED UP" BY VARYING THE QUANTITY AND TYPES OF CHILES USED. TO HELP QUENCH THE FIRE, BE SURE TO OFFER SOOTHING DRINKS, CREAMY TOPPINGS, CRACKERS, TORTILLAS, RICE, AND LOTS OF WARM CORNBREAD.

FLAMING FIREHOUSE CHILI

THERE ARE NEARLY AS MANY RECIPES FOR FIREHOUSE CHILI AS THERE ARE FIREHOUSES. THE VERSATILITY AND EASE OF PREPARATION OF THIS ONE-POT MEAL MAKES CHILI A PERENNIAL FAVORITE AMONG FIREHOUSE COOKS. SERVE THIS ONE WITH CORN-BREAD, AND OFFER A CHOICE OF TOPPINGS.

2 tablespoons olive oil
1 cup chopped onion
2 garlic cloves, minced
1 package (12-ounce) cooked ground beef alternative
    (page 12)
1 can (28-ounce) whole tomatoes, chopped
4 tablespoons hot chili powder (page 7)
1 teaspoon ground cumin
1 teaspoon salt
1½ cups hot salsa
1 cup water
3 cups cooked kidney beans

Heat the oil in a large chili pot over medium heat. Add the onion and garlic, cover, and cook until softened, about 5 minutes. Add the ground beef alternative, tomatoes, chili powder, cumin, salt, salsa, and water. Bring to a boil, lower the heat, and simmer 30 minutes, stirring occasionally. Add the kidney beans, and simmer 15 minutes longer to heat through and blend flavors. Add more water, if necessary, until desired consistency is reached.

SERVES 6

SASSY SALSA CHILI

THIS CHILI IS ESPECIALLY QUICK AND CONVENIENT WHEN MADE WITH BOTTLED SALSA AND CANNED BEANS. TO OFFSET THE HEAT, A BED OF RICE IS STRONGLY RECOMMENDED, ALONG WITH A BOWL OF SOUR CREAM (DAIRY OR NON-DAIRY) ON THE SIDE.

2½ cups textured soy protein granules
2 tablespoons safflower oil
1 large onion, chopped
2 cups hot salsa
1 can (6-ounce) tomato paste
2 tablespoons tamari sauce
4 tablespoons hot chili powder (page 7)
2 teaspoons brown sugar
3 cups cooked pinto beans
2 cups water

Reconstitute the soy granules in water according to package directions, and set aside. Heat the oil in a large chili pot over medium heat. Add the onion, cover, and cook until softened, about 5 minutes. Stir in the salsa, tomato paste, tamari, chili powder, brown sugar, pinto beans, water, and the reserved soy granules. Bring to a boil, lower the heat, and simmer 45 minutes, stirring occasionally. Add more water if the chili becomes too dry.

SERVES 6

Anything But Water...

If your burn alarm goes off while you're eating a bowl of spicy chili, try something creamy or starchy to break down the capsaicin oil that contains the chile heat. Dairy or non-dairy sour cream, yogurt, milk, buttermilk, beer, guacamole, rice, bread, pasta, and tortillas are all popular "pain relievers." Anything but water — the capsaicin is not water soluble and water will have little if any effect in putting out the fire.

BEER CHASER CHILI

BEER IS AN INGREDIENT IN THIS HOT AND HEARTY CHILI, BUT IT ALSO MAKES A GREAT CHASER TO HAVE ON HAND TO DOUSE THE FIRE OF THIS INCENDIARY DISH. THE COOKED GROUND BEEF ALTERNATIVE IS ESPECIALLY FLAVORFUL IN THIS RECIPE. IF GROUND DRIED CHILES ARE UNAVAILABLE, SUBSTITUTE A CHILI POWDER BLEND, CUTTING BACK ON THE ADDITIONAL CUMIN ACCORDING TO TASTE.

1½ tablespoons safflower oil
6 tablespoons ground dried red chiles
1 tablespoon ground cumin
3 garlic cloves, chopped fine
2 medium onions, chopped
1 teaspoon dried oregano, preferably Mexican
1 teaspoon paprika
1 tablespoon cider vinegar
1 can (12-ounce) beer
1 can (4-ounce) diced green chiles, drained
3 cups cooked pinto beans
1 can (14-ounce) stewed tomatoes
1 package (12-ounce) ground beef alternative
  (page 12)
1 teaspoon hot pepper sauce
1 cup water
Salt and fresh-ground black pepper to taste

Heat the oil in a large chili pot over medium heat. Add the ground chiles, cumin, garlic, and onions. Cover, and cook until softened, about 5 minutes. Add the oregano and paprika, and stir to coat. Add the vinegar, beer, diced chiles, pinto beans, tomatoes, ground beef alternative, hot pepper sauce, water, and salt and pepper. Bring to a boil, lower the heat, and simmer, uncovered, for 45 minutes, stirring often.

SERVES 6

HEAT WAVE CHILI

APPLE JUICE AND ASIAN CHILI PASTE ARE THE "SECRET INGRE-DIENTS" IN THIS HOT BUT IRRESISTIBLY TASTY CHILI. BE SURE TO HAVE AN ASSORTMENT OF QUENCHING COOL-DOWNS AT THE READY. USE A GRATER WITH LARGE HOLES TO GRATE THE TEMPEH, TO GIVE IT A TEXTURE SIMILAR TO COARSE GROUND BEEF.

2 tablespoons safflower oil
3 cups grated tempeh
1 medium onion, chopped
½ cup chopped celery
3 garlic cloves, minced
2 tablespoons hot chili powder (page 7)
2 cups diced tomatoes, fresh or canned
1 cup apple juice
1 cup water
2 tablespoons tamari sauce
2 tablespoons tomato paste
2 teaspoons Asian chili paste
2 teaspoons light brown sugar
2 cups cooked red kidney beans

Heat 1 tablespoon of the oil in a skillet over medium heat. Add the tempeh, and cook until browned, about 5 minutes. Set aside.

Heat the remaining oil in a large chili pot over medium heat. Add the onion, celery, and garlic, cover, and cook until the onion is softened, about 5 minutes. Add the chili powder, and stir to coat vegetables. Add the tomatoes, apple juice,

water, tamari, tomato paste, chili paste, brown sugar, and reserved tempeh. Bring to a boil, lower the heat, and simmer, covered, for 20 minutes. Add the kidney beans, and simmer, uncovered, for 20 minutes longer.

SERVES 4

A Matter of Taste

Why do some people like their chili blazing hot, while others think even the mildest chili is too spicy? It could have to do with taste buds. About 50 percent of the population has a "normal" amount of taste buds, and a full 25 percent ("supertasters") have nearly twice the amount of taste buds. The remaining 25 percent — the "non-tasters" — have a very low number of taste buds. This may explain why some people shy away from spicy foods, and others can eat hot chiles as if they were candies.

DEVIL'S FOOD CHILI

VEGETARIAN SAUSAGE COMES IN MANY VARIETIES: FROZEN PRE-COOKED "CRUMBLES," LIGHTLY SEASONED PATTIES, AND MILD OR HOT LINKS. THE CHOPPED JALAPEÑOS MAKE THIS CHILI DEV-ILISHLY HOT AND SPICY. A SOOTHING GUACAMOLE MAKES A GOOD ACCOMPANIMENT.

2 tablespoons olive oil
1 large onion, chopped
3 garlic cloves, minced
4 jalapeños, seeded and chopped
2 cans (28-ounce) whole tomatoes, diced
1 can (6-ounce) tomato paste
1 cup dry red wine
1 cup water
4 tablespoons hot chili powder (page 7)
1 teaspoon salt
¼ teaspoon cayenne
1 pound cooked vegetarian sausage, crumbled
3 cups cooked black beans

Heat the oil in a large chili pot over medium heat. Add the onion, garlic, and jalapeños, cover, and cook until soft-ened, about 5 minutes. Add the tomatoes, tomato paste, red wine, water, chili powder, salt, and cayenne. Bring to a boil,

lower the heat, and simmer, covered, for 15 minutes. Add the vegetarian sausage and black beans, and simmer, uncovered, 30 minutes longer, stirring occasionally.

SERVES 6

GARLIC LOVER'S CHILI

🌶 🌶 🌶

THE ABUNDANCE OF GARLIC COMBINED WITH THE OTHER SPICES ADDS TO THE RICH COMPLEXITY OF FLAVOR IN THIS DELICIOUS CHILI. I LIKE TO SERVE IT OVER PASTA OR WITH HOT, CRUSTY GARLIC BREAD AND A SALAD.

2 tablespoons olive oil
1 pound tempeh, chopped
1 medium onion, chopped
8 garlic cloves, minced
4 tablespoons hot chili powder (page 7)
2 cans (28-ounce) whole tomatoes, chopped
1 can (6-ounce) tomato paste
2 cups water or vegetable stock
1 can (4-ounce) green chiles, chopped
1 tablespoon brown sugar
1 tablespoon dried oregano, preferably Mexican
1 teaspoon cinnamon
½ teaspoon red pepper flakes
¾ teaspoon salt
¼ teaspoon fresh-ground black pepper
3 cups cooked dark-red kidney beans
1 cup sliced ripe olives (or olivada; see page 60)

Heat 1 tablespoon of the oil in a skillet over medium heat. Add the tempeh, and cook until browned, about 5

minutes. Set aside.

Heat the remaining oil in a large chili pot over medium heat. Add the onion, garlic, and chili powder, cover, and cook until softened, about 5 minutes. Add the tomatoes, tomato paste, water, chiles, brown sugar, oregano, cinnamon, red pepper flakes, salt, and pepper. Bring to a boil, lower the heat, and simmer 10 minutes. Add the kidney beans and the reserved tempeh, and simmer 30 minutes longer. Just prior to serving, add the olives and heat through, or swirl a spoonful of olivada into each serving.

SERVES 6

ROASTED RED PEPPER CHILI

AS RELENTLESS IN ITS SPICY HEAT AS IT IS IN ITS FLAVORFUL RICHNESS, OWING TO THE DRY RED WINE AND ROASTED RED PEPPERS, THIS CHILI WILL HAVE YOU COMING BACK FOR MORE. FOR CONVENIENCE, USE JARRED ROASTED RED PEPPERS. CORNBREAD IS A GOOD ACCOMPANIMENT.

1 tablespoon olive oil
1 large onion, chopped
2 garlic cloves, minced
3 jalapeños, seeded and minced
4 tablespoons hot chili powder (page 7)
1 cup dry red wine
1 cup water
2 cups canned crushed tomatoes
Salt and fresh-ground black pepper to taste
1 package (12-ounce) cooked ground beef alternative
   (page 12)
1 jar (10-ounce) roasted red peppers, chopped coarse
3 cups cooked pinto beans

Heat the oil in a large chili pot over medium heat. Add the onion, garlic, and jalapeños, cover, and cook until softened, about 5 minutes. Stir in the chili powder, red wine, water, tomatoes, and salt and pepper. Bring to a boil, lower the heat, and simmer 20 minutes. Stir in the ground beef alternative, roasted red peppers, and pinto beans, and simmer 30 minutes longer.

SERVES 6

SEARING SANTA FE CHILI

THIS POTENT CHILI IS PREPARED NEW MEXICO-STYLE, WITH RED CHILI PODS THAT ARE PURÉED INTO A PASTE. TEXTURED SOY PROTEIN CHUNKS STAND IN FOR THE CUBED MEAT, BUT DICED SEITAN MAY BE USED IF YOU PREFER.

2½ cups textured soy protein chunks
4 ounces dried red chile pods
3½ cups water
2 tablespoons olive oil
1 large onion, chopped
1 garlic clove, minced
1 teaspoon ground cumin
1 teaspoon dried oregano, preferably Mexican
1 teaspoon salt
½ teaspoon fresh-ground black pepper

Reconstitute the soy chunks in water according to package directions, and set aside. Cut the chiles open with a

sharp knife or scissors, and remove the seeds. Rinse the chiles in cold water, cut into small pieces, and place in a medium bowl. Bring 1½ cups of the water to a boil, pour it over the chiles, and cover the bowl with a towel. When the water has cooled, drain the chiles, making sure to reserve the water. Transfer the softened chiles to a food processor, and process with short pulses to make a smooth purée, adding small amounts of the reserved liquid if necessary. Strain the puréed chile mixture through a sieve, and set aside.

Heat the oil in a large chili pot over medium heat. Add the onion and garlic, cover, and cook until softened, about 5 minutes. Add the reserved soy chunks, chile purée, cumin, oregano, salt, and pepper. Cook 5 minutes, stirring frequently. Add the remaining 2 cups water. Bring to a boil, lower the heat, and simmer 1 hour, or until the sauce has thickened. Taste, and adjust seasonings.

SERVES 4 TO 6

TEXAS TOO-HOT CHILI WITH CILANTRO SOUR CREAM

TEXAS CHILI OFTEN CONTAINS TWO KINDS OF MEAT, ONE CUBED AND THE OTHER GROUND. HERE CUBED SEITAN AND CRUMBLED VEGETARIAN SAUSAGE PROVIDE THE TASTE AND TEXTURE VARIATIONS.

1 cup sour cream (dairy or non-dairy)
¼ cup minced fresh cilantro
½ teaspoon salt
2 tablespoons olive oil
8 ounces seitan, cut into ½-inch cubes
1 medium onion, minced
4 tablespoons hot chili powder (page 7)
1 teaspoon dried oregano, preferably Mexican
½ teaspoon ground cumin
Salt and fresh-ground black pepper to taste
1 can (6-ounce) tomato paste
1 cup beer
1 cup water
1 pound cooked vegetarian sausage, crumbled

In a small bowl, combine the sour cream, cilantro, and salt, and mix well. Set aside in the refrigerator.

Heat 1 tablespoon of the oil in a large skillet over medium heat. Add the seitan, and cook until browned on all sides, about 10 minutes. Set aside.

Heat the remaining oil in a large chili pot over medium heat. Add the onion, chili powder, oregano, cumin, and salt and pepper. Cover and cook until softened, about 5 minutes. Add the tomato paste, beer, and water. Bring to a boil, lower

Eat Chili to Keep Cool

Did you know that consuming spicy foods can actually cool you down in hot weather? The capsaicin in chiles dilates the blood vessels, increases blood circulation, and allows the body to perspire more. This throws off heat, since perspiration is the body's natural cooling system. Is it any wonder that spicy foods always seem to come from cultures whose people live in hot climates?

the heat, and simmer, covered, for 30 minutes. Add the reserved seitan and vegetarian sausage, and simmer, uncovered, for 10 minutes longer. Ladle the chili into bowls, with a dollop of the reserved cilantro sour cream on each.

SERVES 6

RED-HOT CHILI WITH CORNBREAD

CORN AND BEANS ARE A STAPLE OF SOUTH AMERICAN CUISINE, AND THEY ALSO COMPLEMENT EACH OTHER NUTRITIONALLY. THE SOOTHING TASTE OF CORNBREAD IS A WELCOME ACCOMPANIMENT TO THIS HOT BUT FLAVORFUL CHILI. LADLE THE CHILI DIRECTLY OVER CORNBREAD, OR SERVE IT SEPARATELY.

1 tablespoon safflower oil
1 medium onion, diced
2 garlic cloves, chopped
2 jalapeños, seeded and minced
4 tablespoons hot chili powder (page 7)
1 teaspoon ground cumin
1 teaspoon paprika
2 cups hot salsa
1 cup water
Salt to taste
1 package (12-ounce) cooked ground beef alternative
   (page 12)
2 cups cooked pinto beans
Cornbread (recipe follows)

Heat the oil in a large chili pot over medium heat. Add the onion and garlic, cover, and cook until softened, about 5 minutes. Add the jalapeños, chili powder, cumin, paprika, salsa, water, and salt. Bring to a boil, lower the heat, and simmer 15 minutes. Add the ground beef alternative and pinto beans, and simmer 20 minutes longer, or until desired flavor and consistency are reached. Serve with warm cornbread.

SERVES 6

CORNBREAD

1 cup yellow cornmeal
1 cup unbleached all-purpose flour
2 teaspoons baking powder
1 teaspoon salt
3 tablespoons corn oil
1 tablespoon honey (or other natural sweetener)
1 cup milk or soy milk
1 cup fresh, frozen, or canned corn kernels, or
  creamed corn

Preheat the oven to 350°F. Oil an 8-inch baking pan or cast-iron skillet.

In a large bowl, combine the cornmeal, flour, baking powder, and salt, and set aside. In a small bowl, combine the oil, honey, milk, and corn, and mix well. Stir the liquid ingredients into the dry ingredients, and mix until just combined. Transfer the batter to the oiled pan or skillet, and bake for 20 to 30 minutes, or until the cornbread is light brown on top and a toothpick inserted in the center comes out clean. Remove from oven, and allow to cool for several minutes before serving.

SERVES 6

BACKYARD BARBECUE CHILI

Chile Fact

An ancho chile is a dried poblano. The Spanish word ancho means "broad" or "wide," which describes this chile's shape. It has a sweet, fruity flavor, and is generally the mild chile used in chili powders.

THE SMOKY SWEETNESS OF BARBECUE SAUCE ADDS A RICH TASTE TO THIS FLAVORFUL CHILI. TO KEEP IN THE BACKYARD BARBECUE SPIRIT, SERVE IT WITH COLESLAW, CORN CHIPS, AND OTHER PICNIC FARE — EVEN IF IT'S SNOWING OUTSIDE.

1 tablespoon safflower oil
2 medium onions, diced
1 small red bell pepper, diced
3 large tomatoes, diced
2 cups tomato purée
1 cup bottled spicy barbecue sauce
4 tablespoons chili powder, commercial or homemade
 (pages 7-8)
1 teaspoon hot sauce
1 teaspoon light brown sugar
Salt and fresh-ground black pepper to taste
1 package (12-ounce) cooked ground beef alternative
 (page 12)
2 cups cooked kidney beans

Heat the oil in a large chili pot over medium heat. Add the onions and bell pepper, cover, and cook until the onion is softened, about 5 minutes. Stir in the tomatoes, tomato purée, barbecue sauce, chili powder, hot sauce, brown sugar, and salt and pepper. Bring to a boil, adding water if mixture is too thick, lower the heat, and simmer, covered, for 15 minutes, stirring occasionally. Add the ground beef alternative and kidney beans, and simmer 15 minutes longer.

SERVES 6

FOUR-BEAN THREE-ALARM CHILI

MIX AND MATCH BEANS ACCORDING TO YOUR PREFERENCE. THIS RECIPE IS ESPECIALLY SUITED TO USING CANNED BEANS FOR EASE OF PREPARATION. THE SMOKY TASTE OF THE CHIPOTLE CHILE COMPLEMENTS THE FLAVOR OF THE BEANS.

1 tablespoon safflower oil
1 medium onion, chopped
4 tablespoons hot chili powder (page 7)
1 teaspoon hot pepper sauce
1 teaspoon salt
¼ teaspoon cayenne
3 cups tomato juice
1 chipotle chile, canned in adobo sauce, minced
1½ cups cooked pinto beans
1½ cups cooked dark red kidney beans
1 cup cooked Great Northern beans
1 cup cooked black beans

Heat the oil in a large chili pot over medium heat. Add the onion, cover, and cook until softened, about 5 minutes. Stir in the chili powder, hot pepper sauce, salt, cayenne, tomato juice, and chipotle. Bring to a boil, lower the heat, and simmer 15 minutes. Add the beans, and simmer gently, uncovered, 30 minutes longer. Serve accompanied by your choice of garnishes.

SERVES 6

SPICY VEGETARIAN SAUSAGE AND BEAN CHILI

THE INTENSE FLAVORS OF THE ANCHO PASTE AND SPICY SAUSAGE GIVE THIS CHILI A HEARTY, FULL-BODIED FLAVOR. I LIKE TO USE MORNINGSTAR FARMS SAUSAGE-STYLE RECIPE CRUMBLES IN THIS RECIPE, BUT ANY OTHER VEGETARIAN SAUSAGE WILL DO.

4 dried ancho chiles
3 garlic cloves
1 tablespoon cumin seed
¼ teaspoon cayenne
1 medium onion, chopped
1 tablespoon safflower oil
1 teaspoon dried oregano, preferably Mexican
2 cups tomato purée
Salt and fresh-ground black pepper to taste
1 pound cooked vegetarian sausage, crumbled
2 cups cooked pinto beans

Remove seeds and stems from the chiles. Plunge the chiles into a pot of boiling water, remove immediately, and drain. Place the chiles in a blender or food processor with the garlic, cumin seed, and cayenne. Purée, and set aside.

Heat the oil in a large chili pot over medium heat. Add the onion, cover, and cook until softened, about 5 minutes. Stir in the reserved chili paste, oregano, tomato purée, and salt and pepper. Bring to a boil, lower the heat, and simmer, covered, for 15 minutes. Add the vegetarian sausage and pinto beans, and simmer 30 minutes longer, adding water if the chili is too dry.

SERVES 6

BLAZING THREE-CHILE CHILI

🍅 🍅 🍅

THE SWEETNESS OF THE CORN HELPS TO OFFSET SOME OF THE CHILE HEAT, BUT YOU'LL STILL WANT TO PLAN A FEW "COOL-DOWN" ACCOMPANIMENTS FOR THIS FIERY CHILI. TRUE FIRE-EATERS MAY WANT TO INCREASE THE NUMBER OF CHILES, OR ADD A HABANERO OR SCOTCH BONNET TO THE POT.

🍅

1 tablespoon safflower oil
1 serrano chile, minced
1 jalapeño, minced
3 tablespoons hot chili powder (page 7)
1 teaspoon sugar
1 teaspoon ground cumin
2 cups diced tomatoes, canned or fresh
2 cups fresh or frozen corn kernels
1 can (4-ounce) diced green chiles, drained
1½ cups water or tomato juice
3 cups cooked pinto beans
1 cup grated cheddar or soy cheese, for garnish

🍅

Heat the oil in a large chili pot over medium heat. Add the serrano and jalapeño, cover, and cook until softened, about 5 minutes. Add the chili powder, sugar, cumin, tomatoes, corn, chiles, water or tomato juice, and pinto beans. Bring to a boil, lower the heat, and simmer 30 to 45 minutes, adding more water if mixture becomes too thick. Serve topped with the grated cheese.

SERVES 4

Chile Heat

🍅

As a general rule, the smaller the chile, the hotter it is. The chile's interior membranes contain the most heat, followed by the seeds. Always be careful when removing the seeds, and be sure not to touch your eyes until you have washed your hands thoroughly after working with chiles. Wearing rubber gloves is a wise precaution against coming in contact with the volatile capsaicin oil.

CHILI NUEVO

CHILI GETS A NEW LOOK WITH THIS COLLECTION OF SOPHISTICATED INTERPRETATIONS DESIGNED TO DAZZLE YOUR FAMILY AND FRIENDS. MAKING CHILI HAS A WAY OF BRINGING OUT THE CREATIVITY IN A COOK. A PINCH OF THYME OR A SPLASH OF WINE CAN ADD CHARACTER, AND SOME UNUSUAL INGREDIENTS, SUCH AS ORANGE LIQUEUR, CAN PROVIDE A SPECIAL NUANCE. USE THESE RECIPES AS A SPRINGBOARD FOR YOUR OWN INVENTIVE SPIRIT. PREPARE ONE AT YOUR NEXT PARTY, OR JUST WHEN YOU WANT TO TRY SOMETHING DIFFERENT. IN ADDITION TO SOPHISTICATED PARTY FOOD, THIS CHAPTER ALSO CONTAINS SOME QUICK AND EASY RECIPES MADE WITH ON-HAND INGREDIENTS AND NO CHOPPING OR DICING.

SPICY APPLE-RAISIN CHILI

THE ADDITION OF FRUIT MAKES THIS CHILI SLIGHTLY SWEET AND VERY SATISFYING. IT IS ESPECIALLY GOOD TOPPED WITH SOUR CREAM OR YOGURT, WHETHER REGULAR, LOW-FAT, OR DAIRY-FREE.

1½ tablespoons safflower oil
2 medium onions, chopped
1 medium carrot, chopped
½ cup chopped celery
2 garlic cloves, minced
1 Granny Smith apple, peeled, cored, and chopped
4 tablespoons mild chili powder (page 8)
2 cups apple juice
2 teaspoons light brown sugar
1 teaspoon cinnamon
1 can (16-ounce) plum tomatoes, chopped
1 can (4-ounce) mild green chiles, chopped
1 teaspoon salt
⅛ teaspoon fresh-ground black pepper
4 cups cooked black beans
½ cup raisins

Heat the oil in a large chili pot over medium heat. Add the onions, carrot, celery, and garlic. Cover, and cook until the onion is softened, about 5 minutes. Add the apple, chili powder, apple juice, brown sugar, cinnamon, tomatoes, chiles, salt, and pepper. Bring to a boil, lower the heat, and simmer, covered, for 20 minutes, stirring occasionally. Add the black beans and raisins, and simmer 20 minutes longer, or until flavors are well blended and desired consistency is reached.

SERVES 6

LENTIL CHILI WITH COUSCOUS

🍅 🍅 🍅

LENTILS ARE POPULAR IN THE UNITED STATES, AS WELL AS IN EUROPE, INDIA, AND THE MIDDLE EAST. THEY ARE RICH IN CALCIUM, POTASSIUM, ZINC, AND IRON. THIS LENTIL CHILI MAKES GREAT COMPANY FARE — NOT TOO HOT, BUT FULL OF FLAVOR. ACCOMPANIMENTS MIGHT INCLUDE SEPARATE BOWLS OF CRUSHED PEANUTS, GOLDEN RAISINS, AND CHUTNEY.

2 tablespoons olive oil
1 large onion, chopped
1 carrot, chopped
1 red bell pepper, chopped
2 garlic cloves, minced
2 cups lentils, picked over and rinsed
1 can (28-ounce) crushed tomatoes
1 bay leaf
3 tablespoons mild chili powder (page 8)
1 teaspoon salt
1 teaspoon dried marjoram
2 cups tomato juice
3 cups salted water or vegetable stock
1½ cups couscous
2 tablespoons minced scallions
2 tablespoons minced parsley or cilantro

Heat the oil in a large pot over medium heat. Add the onion, carrot, bell pepper, and garlic. Cover, and cook until the onion is softened, about 5 minutes. Add the lentils and enough water to cover the lentils by one inch. Bring to a boil, lower the heat, and simmer, covered, for 30 minutes, or until the lentils are tender. Add the tomatoes, bay leaf, chili powder, salt, marjoram, and tomato juice, and simmer for 15 minutes, stirring occasionally. If the mixture becomes too dry, add a small amount of water. (Be sure to remove the bay leaf from the chili before serving.)

While the chili is simmering, prepare the couscous: Bring the 3 cups salted water or stock to a boil in a medium saucepan. Add the couscous and 1 tablespoon each of the scallions and parsley, cover, and remove the pan from the heat. Allow the couscous to sit for 5 minutes. Serve the couscous in a shallow bowl or serving dish, with the chili on top and garnished with the remaining scallions and parsley.

SERVES 6

GOLDEN GARBANZO CHILI

GARBANZO IS THE SPANISH NAME FOR CHICKPEA, THE MEATY, NUTRITIOUS BEAN THAT IS SO POPULAR WORLDWIDE. THIS MILD, BRIGHTLY COLORED CHILI IS PLEASING TO THE EYE AS WELL AS THE PALATE.

1 tablespoon olive oil
1 medium onion, chopped
1 large yellow bell pepper, chopped
2 garlic cloves, minced
1 can (28-ounce) crushed tomatoes
2 tablespoons mild chili powder (page 8)
1 teaspoon salt
1 teaspoon light brown sugar
⅛ teaspoon turmeric
1 cup water
1 cup apple juice
3 cups cooked garbanzos or chickpeas
2 tablespoons minced parsley

eat the oil in a large skillet over medium heat. Add the onion, bell pepper, and garlic, cover, and cook until the onion is softened, about 5 minutes. Add the tomatoes, chili powder, salt, brown sugar, turmeric, water, and apple juice. Bring to a boil, lower the heat, and simmer 15 minutes. Add the garbanzos, and simmer 30 minutes longer, stirring occasionally. Taste, and adjust seasonings. Serve the chili sprinkled with the parsley.

SERVES 4

IMPROMPTU PARTY CHILI

THIS IS A RICH, FLAVORFUL CHILI THAT TASTES LIKE IT TOOK ALL DAY TO PREPARE BUT PULLS TOGETHER IN A SNAP WITH INGREDIENTS FROM YOUR PANTRY. THE BITS OF ONION, BELL PEPPER, AND CELERY IN THE SALSA SAVE YOU THE STEP OF CHOPPING FRESH VEGETABLES.

2 cups chunky salsa
4 tablespoons chili powder, commercial or homemade
  (pages 7-8)
1 can (4-ounce) chopped green chiles
1 can (6-ounce) tomato paste
2 cups water
1 package (12-ounce) cooked ground beef alternative
  (page 12)
2 cans (16-ounce) pinto beans
Salt and fresh-ground black pepper to taste

In a large chili pot over medium heat, mix the salsa and chili powder until well blended. Add the green chiles, tomato paste, and water, and stir well. Bring to a boil, lower the heat, and simmer 30 minutes, stirring often. Add the ground beef alternative, pinto beans, and salt and pepper, and simmer 15 minutes longer to heat through and thicken. Serve with your favorite accompaniments.

SERVES 6

WHITE BEAN AND SAUSAGE CHILI

THE RICH, CREAMY TASTE OF THE CANNELLINI BEANS IS THE PERFECT FOIL FOR THE SPICE OF THE VEGETARIAN SAUSAGE AND OTHER CHILI SEASONINGS. I LIKE TO SERVE THIS CHILI WITH A LOAF OF HOT CRUSTY ITALIAN BREAD AND A CRISP GREEN SALAD.

2 tablespoons olive oil
2 cups chopped onion
2 garlic cloves, minced
4 tablespoons chili powder, commercial or homemade
    (pages 7-8)
1 teaspoon ground cumin
1 can (28-ounce) crushed tomatoes
1 cup water
1 tablespoon vegetarian Worcestershire sauce
¼ teaspoon ground sage
¾ teaspoon salt
⅛ teaspoon fresh-ground black pepper
1 pound cooked vegetarian sausage, crumbled
3 cups cooked cannellini beans

Heat the oil in a large chili pot over medium heat. Add the onion and garlic, cover, and cook until softened, about 5 minutes. Add the chili powder, cumin, tomatoes, water, Worcestershire sauce, sage, salt, and pepper. Bring to a boil, lower the heat, and simmer 40 minutes. Add the vegetarian sausage and cannellini beans, and simmer, uncovered, for 20 minutes longer, adding more water if the chili becomes too dry.

SERVES 6

ORANGE-AND-THYME-SCENTED CHILI

THIS RICH, AROMATIC CHILI IS ONE OF MY PERSONAL FAVORITES. FRAGRANT WITH ORANGE AND THYME, IT IS SOPHISTICATED ENOUGH TO SERVE AT A DINNER PARTY. TRY IT SERVED OVER BASMATI RICE, ACCOMPANIED BY A CRISP WHITE WINE.

1 tablespoon safflower oil
1 large onion, chopped
1 red bell pepper, chopped
l jalapeño chile, minced
3 tablespoons chili powder, commercial or homemade
    (pages 7-8)
1 tablespoon minced fresh thyme, or 1 teaspoon dried
1 teaspoon paprika
1 tablespoon light brown sugar
1 can (15-ounce) diced tomatoes
1 cup hot or mild salsa
3 cups cooked black beans
1 pound cooked vegetarian sausage, crumbled
1 cup fresh-squeezed orange juice

2 tablespoons orange liqueur (optional)
1 tablespoon orange zest
Sour cream, orange slices, and thyme sprigs, for garnish

Heat the oil in a large chili pot over medium heat. Add the onion, red bell pepper, and jalapeño, cover, and cook until the onion is softened, about 5 minutes. Stir in the chili powder, thyme, paprika, and brown sugar. Add the tomatoes, salsa, black beans, and vegetarian sausage, lower the heat, and simmer 20 minutes. Add the orange juice, liqueur, and orange zest, and simmer 15 minutes longer, adding a little water if the chili becomes too dry. Serve the chili garnished with the sour cream, orange slices, and thyme sprigs.

SERVES 6

CHILI BORRACHA

●●●

THIS "DRUNKEN CHILI" INCLUDES THE INGREDIENTS FOR A "BOILERMAKER" — A SHOT OF WHISKEY DROPPED IN A GLASS OF BEER AND THEN CHUGGED ALL AT ONCE. BUT INSTEAD OF CHUGGING THIS CHILI, YOU'LL WANT TO SLOWLY SAVOR IT.

2½ cups textured soy protein granules
1 tablespoon olive oil
1 large onion, chopped
2 garlic cloves, minced
1 can (28-ounce) whole tomatoes
1 can (28-ounce) tomato purée
1 cup beer
3 tablespoons whiskey
3 tablespoons chili powder, commercial or homemade
   (pages 7-8)
1 tablespoon unsweetened cocoa
Salt to taste
3 cups cooked pinto beans

Reconstitute the soy granules in water according to package directions, and set aside. Heat the oil in a large chili pot over medium heat. Add the onion and garlic, cover, and cook until softened, about 5 minutes. Add the tomatoes, purée, beer, whiskey, chili powder, and cocoa. Bring to a boil, lower the heat, add the reserved soy granules, and simmer 30 minutes. Add the salt and pinto beans, and simmer 15 minutes longer.

SERVES 6

CHILI JAVA

THE ADDITION OF STRONG BLACK COFFEE ADDS A HEARTY RICH-NESS TO THIS CHILI. IT IS SAID THAT CHUCKWAGON COOKS OF THE OLD WEST OFTEN USED LEFTOVER COFFEE IN THEIR COOK-ING TO CONSERVE THEIR SUPPLY OF FRESH WATER.

A True Chile Chili Bean

Isn't it interesting that a bean from *Chile* is also a popular bean in chili, and that they both arrived on the scene at the same time? It is said that kidney beans came to the United States from the country of Chile during the time of the gold rush in the mid-nineteenth century — the same time period that many authorities fix the origin of chili.

2½ cups textured soy protein granules
1 tablespoon olive oil
1 medium onion, chopped
2 garlic cloves, minced
3 tablespoons chili powder, commercial or homemade
  (pages 7-8)
1 teaspoon ground cumin
1 cup strong-brewed coffee
1 cup water
3 cups cooked dark red kidney beans
1 can (4-ounce) diced green chiles
2 tablespoons lime juice
1 tablespoon chopped cilantro
Salt and fresh-ground black pepper to taste
Regular or low-fat sour cream (dairy or non-dairy),
  for garnish

Reconstitute the soy granules in water according to package directions, and set aside. Heat the oil in a large chili pot over medium heat. Add the onion and garlic, cover, and cook until softened, about 5 minutes. Stir in the chili powder, cumin, coffee, and water. Bring to a boil, lower the heat, add the reserved soy granules, kidney beans, and green chiles, and simmer 35 to 40 minutes. Stir in the lime juice, cilantro, and salt and pepper, and simmer 5 minutes longer. To serve, top each serving with a dollop of the sour cream.

SERVES 6

TEQUILA SUNDOWN CHILI

EQUILA AND LIME DELIVER A PUNGENT KICK AND ORANGE
JUICE ADDS A SUBTLE SWEETNESS TO THIS PARTY CHILI. SERVE
IT WITH YOUR FAVORITE TOPPINGS AND SIDE DISHES, ALONG
WITH A PITCHER OF TEQUILA SUNRISES, OR MAYBE SOME COLD
BEER SERVED IN GLASSES RIMMED WITH LIME JUICE AND SEA SALT.

2 tablespoons olive oil
2 cups chopped onion
2 garlic cloves, minced
2 tablespoons chili powder, commercial or homemade
    (pages 7-8)
1 teaspoon ground coriander
2 cups diced tomatoes, fresh or canned
¼ cup tomato paste
¼ cup tequila
2 tablespoons lime juice
¼ cup orange juice
1 cup water
2 teaspoons dried savory
1 teaspoon salt
¼ teaspoon fresh-ground black pepper
1 tablespoon sugar
4 cups cooked pinto beans

eat the oil in a large pot over medium heat. Add the onion,
garlic, chili powder, and coriander. Cover, and cook until
softened, about 5 minutes. Stir in the tomatoes, tomato
paste, tequila, lime juice, orange juice, water, savory, salt,
pepper, and sugar. Bring to a boil, lower the heat, and simmer
15 minutes, stirring occasionally. Add the pinto beans, and
simmer 30 minutes longer, or until desired consistency is
reached.

SERVES 6

FIFTEEN-BEAN CHILI

THIS RECIPE STARTS WITH THE DRIED BEANS THAT HAVE BEEN PACKAGED AS "15 BEAN SOUP," WHICH ARE WIDELY AVAILABLE IN THE DRIED BEAN SECTION OF MOST SUPERMARKETS. THE RESULT IS A FLAVORFUL, MULTI-TEXTURED CHILI.

1 package (16-ounce) dried "15 bean soup" beans
1 tablespoon safflower oil
1 cup chopped onion
2 garlic cloves, minced
4 tablespoons hot or mild chili powder (pages 7-8)
1 teaspoon ground cumin
1 teaspoon dried oregano, preferably Mexican
Salt and fresh-ground black pepper to taste
1½ cups diced tomatoes, fresh or canned
1 can (6-ounce) tomato paste
2 cups water
Sour cream (dairy or non-dairy), diced avocado, and salsa, as accompaniments

Soak the beans in water overnight. Cook the beans in water according to package directions, or until soft, and set aside.

Heat the oil in a large chili pot over medium heat. Add the onion and garlic, cover, and cook until softened, about 5 minutes. Add the chili powder, cumin, oregano, and salt and pepper. Stir in the tomatoes, tomato paste, and water. Bring to a boil, lower the heat, and simmer 15 minutes. Add the reserved beans, and simmer 30 minutes longer, or until desired consistency is reached. To serve, ladle the chili into bowls, and top with the sour cream, diced avocado, and salsa.

SERVES 6

JON'S "NO-BULL" CHILI

My husband, Jon, loves to cook, and chili is one of his specialties. His recipe secrets include frying off the tomato paste to remove the bitterness, and adding a Vidalia onion and a carrot for natural sweetness. This recipe makes a thick, dark-red chili. Served over brown rice, it is as healthful as it is delicious.

3 tablespoons canola oil
1 cup chopped celery
1 medium carrot, chopped
1 Vidalia onion (or other sweet onion), chopped
3 tablespoons chili powder, commercial or homemade
   (pages 7-8)
1 can (6-ounce) tomato paste
1 can (28-ounce) whole tomatoes, diced
1 can (28-ounce) tomato sauce
1½ cups water
¼ teaspoon cayenne
Salt and fresh-ground black pepper to taste
2 cans (15½-ounce) red kidney beans, rinsed
1 package (12-ounce) cooked ground beef alternative
   (page 12)

Heat 2 tablespoons of the canola oil in a large chili pot over medium heat. Add the celery, carrot, onion, and chili powder, cover, and cook until the onion is softened, about 5 to 10 minutes.

While the vegetables are cooking, heat the remaining 1 tablespoon oil in a small sauté pan over medium heat. Add the tomato paste, and fry it gently for 2 minutes, turning with a spatula and taking care not to burn it. Transfer the fried tomato paste to the chili pot, along with the tomatoes, tomato

sauce, water, cayenne, salt and pepper, kidney beans, and ground beef alternative, and mix thoroughly. Lower the heat, and simmer 45 minutes, stirring occasionally.

SERVES 6

NO BEANS ABOUT IT CHILI

🍅 🍅 🍅

THIS MILD, SLIGHTLY SWEET, BEAN-LESS CHILI IS A FAVORITE WITH CHILDREN. SERVE IT IN TORTILLA "BOWLS" (SEE SIDEBAR) WITH AN ASSORTMENT OF YOUR FAVORITE CONDIMENTS ON THE TABLE.

🍅

2½ cups textured soy protein granules
1 tablespoon safflower oil
1 medium onion, chopped
2 cans (28-ounce) plum tomatoes
1 tablespoon brown sugar
1 tablespoon cider vinegar
4 tablespoons mild chili powder (page 8)
Salt and fresh-ground black pepper to taste
2 cups apple juice

🍅

Rehydrate the soy granules in water according to package directions, and set aside. Heat the oil in a large chili pot over medium heat. Add the onion, cover, and cook until softened, about 5 minutes. Add the reserved soy granules, tomatoes, brown sugar, vinegar, chili powder, and salt and pepper. Stir in the apple juice, lower the heat, and simmer 30 to 40 minutes, or until vegetables are tender and desired consistency is reached.

SERVES 6

Edible Chili Bowls

🌶

For a fun change of pace, make tortilla bowls to hold your chili. Press 8-inch flour tortillas into small microwaveable bowls, and microwave on high for about 2 minutes. Carefully remove the tortilla "bowls" from their molds, and allow them to cool before filling them with prepared chili.

CHILI WITH CHOCOLATE

THIS SUBSTANTIAL CHILI HAS A RICH DEPTH OF FLAVOR DUE TO THE UNSWEETENED CHOCOLATE, WHICH BALANCES THE ACIDITY OF THE TOMATOES. PUMPKIN SEEDS AND SHAVED CHOCO- LATE APPEAR AS INTERESTING AND FLAVORFUL GARNISHES.

1 tablespoon olive oil
1 large onion, chopped
1 medium carrot, chopped fine
2 garlic cloves, minced
3 tablespoons chili powder, commercial or homemade
    (pages 7-8)
1 tablespoon ground cumin
1 teaspoon dried savory
1 teaspoon sugar
1 ounce unsweetened chocolate, chopped coarse
1 cup water
1 cup apple juice
3 cups cooked pinto beans
1 can (4-ounce) diced green chiles
1 package (12-ounce) cooked ground beef alternative
    (page 12)
Salt and fresh-ground black pepper to taste
Pumpkin seeds and shaved chocolate,
    for garnish

Heat the oil in a large chili pot over medium heat. Add the onion, carrot, and garlic, cover, and cook until softened, about 10 minutes. Add the chili powder, cumin, savory, sugar, unsweetened chocolate, water, and apple juice. Bring to a boil, lower the heat, and simmer 15 minutes. Add the pinto beans, chiles, ground beef alternative, and salt and pepper. Simmer, uncovered, stirring occasionally, for 30 minutes, or

until the chili thickens and the flavors have time to develop. Garnish each serving with the pumpkin seeds and shaved chocolate.

SERVES 6

CHIPOTLE CHILI WITH RED WINE AND SEITAN

CANNED CHIPOTLE CHILES IN *ADOBO* SAUCE ADD A SMOKY RICHNESS TO THIS CHILI. THEY ARE AVAILABLE IN SPECIALTY FOOD SHOPS AND THE MEXICAN FOOD SECTION OF MANY SUPERMARKETS. SERVE A DRY RED WINE TO COMPLEMENT THE WINE IN THE CHILI.

Chile Fact

Chipotles are dried and smoked jalapeños, and are available dried or canned in adobo sauce. Extremely hot and flavorful, they lend a smoky barbecue flavor when used in cooking.

2 tablespoons olive oil
1 pound seitan, cut into ½-inch cubes
1 large onion, diced
2 garlic cloves, minced
1 green bell pepper, chopped
1 small jalapeño, seeded and minced
2 canned chipotle chiles, minced
3 tablespoons chili powder, commercial or homemade
   (pages 7-8)
½ teaspoon dried oregano, preferably Mexican
1 teaspoon salt
1 cup dry red wine
1 cup water
2 cups diced tomatoes, fresh or canned
2 cups cooked kidney beans
1 cup grated Monterey jack or soy cheese, as garnish

Heat 1 tablespoon of the oil in a skillet over medium heat. Add the seitan, and cook until browned on all sides, 6 to 8 minutes. Set aside.

Heat the remaining oil in a large chili pot over medium heat. Add the onion, garlic, bell pepper, jalapeño, chipotles, chili powder, oregano, and salt. Cover, and cook until softened, about 5 minutes. Add the red wine, water, tomatoes, and kidney beans. Bring to a boil, lower the heat, add the reserved seitan, and simmer 45 minutes to cook through and blend flavors. Ladle the chili into bowls, and sprinkle with the grated cheese.

SERVES 6

CAN-DO VEGGIE BURGER CHILI

A CAN OF THIS AND A CAN OF THAT, COMBINED WITH CRUMBLED VEGGIE BURGERS, MAKE THIS EASY CHILI A FAVORITE WITH COLLEGE STUDENTS. THE VEGETABLES IN THE CHUNKY SALSA ADD SUBSTANCE AND MAKE CHOPPING VEGETABLES UNNECESSARY. THE CRUMBLED VEGGIE BURGERS GIVE A MEATY TEXTURE AND WORK GREAT IN A PINCH WHEN THERE ARE NO OTHER MEAT ALTERNATIVES IN THE HOUSE.

2 or 3 frozen veggie burgers, thawed
1 tablespoon safflower oil
3 tablespoons chili powder
2 cups chunky salsa
1 can (16-ounce) tomato purée
2 cans (16-ounce) pinto beans, rinsed
1 cup water
Salt and fresh-ground black pepper to taste

A Personal Touch

Use beer, red wine, vegetable stock, or tomato juice to replace all or part of the water in any chili recipe. You can also add a pinch of your favorite spice (perhaps one not normally found in chili, such as mace or curry powder) to put your signature on a chili recipe.

Chop or crumble the veggie burgers. Heat the oil in a large chili pot over medium heat, and add the crumbled veggie burgers. Stir in the chili powder, salsa, tomato purée, pinto beans, water, and salt and pepper, and simmer 30 to 40 minutes. If the chili becomes too thick, add more water. Serve the chili over pasta or rice, accompanied by your favorite toppings.

SERVES 4 TO 6

GREAT WHITE WAY CHILI

WHITE CHILIS, TRADITIONALLY MADE WITH TURKEY OR CHICKEN, SOMETIMES TURN UP AT CHILI COOK-OFFS, ALWAYS TURNING HEADS AND OFTEN WALKING AWAY WITH A PRIZE. THIS VEGGIE VERSION USES TOFU AND HOMINY AND IS SERVED OVER RICE FOR A WHITE-ON-WHITE APPEARANCE. FOR A STRIKING CONTRAST, PRESENT IT IN BRIGHTLY COLORED BOWLS AND GARNISH IT WITH SALSA.

2 tablespoons olive oil
1 large onion, chopped
2 garlic cloves, minced
1 teaspoon dried oregano, preferably Mexican
¾ teaspoon ground cumin
2 cans (4-ounce) green chiles, diced
½ cup dry white wine
1 cup water
1 pound firm tofu, crumbled
2 cans (16-ounce) hominy, rinsed and drained
Salt to taste

Heat the oil in a large chili pot over medium heat. Add the onion and garlic, cover, and cook until softened, about 5 minutes. Add the oregano, cumin, chiles, white wine, and water. Bring to a boil, lower the heat, and simmer 15 minutes. Add the tofu, hominy, and salt, and simmer 20 minutes longer, stirring occasionally. If the chili is too thick, add an additional cup of water. Serve over rice.

SERVES 4 TO 6

FALSE-ALARM CHILI

AN ANCHO CHILE, DARK BROWN IN COLOR AND TRIANGULAR IN SHAPE, IS A POPULAR CHILE IN MEXICAN DISHES. THIS CHILI HAS ALL THE RICH, SPICY FLAVOR YOU'D EXPECT FROM A POT OF CHILI, BUT WITHOUT THE HEAT.

6 dried ancho chiles, seeded
2 cups chopped tomatoes, fresh or canned
2 tablespoons mild chili powder (page 8)
2 teaspoons ground cumin
1 teaspoon paprika
1 teaspoon dried oregano, preferably Mexican
2 teaspoons light brown sugar
2 tablespoons safflower oil
1 large onion, chopped
2 garlic cloves, minced
1 pound seitan, cut into ½-inch cubes
1 cup beer
1 cup water or vegetable stock
2 cups cooked pinto beans

Place the ancho chiles in a small chili pot, and cover them with water. Bring to a boil, lower the heat, and simmer 15 minutes. Remove the pot from the heat, drain the chiles, and cool. In a food processor or blender, combine the drained chiles, tomatoes, chili powder, cumin, paprika, oregano, and brown sugar. Process until smooth, and set aside.

Heat the oil in a large chili pot over medium heat. Add the onion and garlic, cover, and cook until softened, about 5 minutes. Transfer the onion mixture to a small bowl, and set aside. Add the seitan and cook until browned, 6 to 8 minutes, stirring frequently. Add the reserved onion mixture, reserved tomato spice mixture, beer, water, and beans. Bring to a boil, lower the heat, and simmer 45 minutes. Serve with your favorite accompaniments.

SERVES 6

CHILI MARGARITA

W HAT TO SERVE WITH THIS TEQUILA AND LIME JUICE-SPIKED CHILI? WHY, MARGARITAS, OF COURSE!

1 tablespoon olive oil
1 large onion, chopped
1 carrot, chopped
1 red bell pepper, chopped
1 can (28-ounce) crushed tomatoes
3 tablespoons hot chili powder (page 7)
½ teaspoon salt
⅛ teaspoon fresh-ground black pepper
⅓ cup tequila
3 tablespoons fresh-squeezed lime juice
1 cup water
4 cups cooked pinto beans
2 tablespoons minced scallions, for garnish
2 tablespoons minced parsley, for garnish

Heat the oil in a large chili pot over medium heat. Add the onion, carrot, and bell pepper, cover, and cook until the onion is softened, about 5 minutes. Add the tomatoes, chili powder, salt, and pepper. Stir in the tequila, lime juice, water, and pinto beans. Bring to a boil, lower the heat, and simmer 30 minutes, stirring occasionally. Serve garnished with the scallions and parsley.

SERVES 6

SANTI'S AWARD-WINNING FIVE-SPICE CHILI

MY FRIEND SANTI MEUNIER WAS AWARDED "BEST CHILI" IN BERKSHIRE COUNTY, MASSACHUSETTS, FOR THIS TASTE TREAT. THE INGREDIENTS IN THIS SWEET, AROMATIC CHILI HAVE BEEN A CLOSELY GUARDED SECRET UNTIL NOW, BUT LUCKY FOR US, SANTI HAS AGREED TO SHARE HER RECIPE. SERVE THIS CHILI OVER BASMATI RICE, WITH DAIRY OR TOFU SOUR CREAM ON TOP AND CORN MUFFINS ON THE SIDE. FIVE-SPICE POWDER, A BLEND OF AROMATIC SPICES SUCH AS STAR ANISE AND GINGER, CAN BE FOUND IN ASIAN MARKETS OR GOURMET FOOD STORES.

3 tablespoons olive oil
3 medium carrots, chopped fine
1 large sweet onion, chopped
3 tablespoons chili powder, commercial or homemade
*   (pages 7-8)*
1 can (6-ounce) tomato paste
1 cup water
2 cans (28-ounce) chopped tomatoes

2 tablespoons Chinese Five-Spice Powder
¼ teaspoon cayenne
¼ cup dark molasses
1 can (15½-ounce) kidney beans, drained
1 can (15½-ounce) vegetarian baked beans
*   (undrained)*
1 package (12-ounce) cooked ground beef alternative
*   (page 12)*
Salt and fresh-ground black pepper to taste

Heat the oil in a large chili pot over medium heat. Add the carrots, onion, and chili powder, cover, and cook until the onion is softened and the carrots are tender, about 10 minutes. Transfer the mixture to a blender, and grind in short pulses. Add the tomato paste and water to the blender, and purée. Transfer the mixture to the chili pot, and stir in the tomatoes, five-spice powder, cayenne, and molasses. Add the kidney beans, baked beans, ground beef alternative, and salt and pepper. Simmer 45 minutes to an hour, stirring occasionally to prevent the chili from burning. Add an additional cup of water if a thinner chili is desired.

SERVES 6

MADE WITH CHILI

THE FULL-BODIED FLAVOR OF CHILI, IN ALL ITS SPICY RICHNESS, MAKES IT THE PERFECT INGREDIENT TO GIVE A LIFT TO AN EVERYDAY MEAL. ADD CHILI TO YOUR CASSEROLE OR SAVORY PIE, BURRITOS OR TACOS, OR USE YOUR IMAGINATION TO CREATE A DISH OF YOUR OWN. ALL THE RECIPES IN THIS CHAPTER CONTAIN CHILI AS A MAIN INGREDIENT TO PRODUCE ANOTHER DISH; THEY ARE GREAT FOR LEFTOVER CHILI. THEY'RE SO GOOD, YOU MAY WANT TO PLAN AHEAD AND SAVE A SERVING FROM YOUR BATCH OF CHILI TO USE HERE.

AVOCADO-CHILI DIP

THIS DIP IS FUN TO SERVE AS "CHILI PARFAITS." INSTEAD OF USING A LARGE SERVING BOWL, SET OUT INDIVIDUAL DESSERT GLASSES AND DIVIDE THE INGREDIENTS EVENLY AMONG THE GLASSES. EACH GUEST WILL HAVE A PERSONAL DIP GOBLET OF THEIR OWN.

2 avocados
1 tablespoon fresh-squeezed lime juice
¼ teaspoon salt
⅛ teaspoon cayenne
2 cups prepared chili, warmed
1 cup salsa
1 can (4-ounce) diced green chiles
½ cup sliced ripe olives
½ cup grated cheddar or soy cheese
Tortilla chips, as accompaniment

Halve and pit the avocados, and scoop the flesh into a food processor. Add the lime juice, salt, and cayenne, and blend until puréed. Spread half of the chili in a layer at the bottom of a serving bowl (preferably clear glass), followed by a layer of all the salsa. Next, add a layer of the avocado mixture, and top it off with a layer of the remaining chili. Spread the diced chiles, olives, and grated cheese over all. Serve with tortilla chips for dipping.

SERVES 6

CHILI SALAD

THIS RECIPE OFFERS A REFRESHING WAY TO STRETCH A FEW CUPS OF CHILI INTO A SATISFYING LUNCH FOR SIX. THIS SALAD IS ALSO GREAT SERVED IN EDIBLE TORTILLA BOWLS (PAGE 95).

6 cups shredded lettuce
3 cups prepared chili, warmed
1 cup salsa
1 cup sour cream (dairy or non-dairy)
1 cup grated cheddar or soy cheese
1 red bell pepper, chopped
1 avocado, diced
¼ cup sliced ripe olives
Tortilla chips, as accompaniment

Place 1 cup of the lettuce on each of six salad plates. Top each with about ½ cup of the chili. In a small bowl, combine the salsa and sour cream, mix well, and spoon evenly over the chili. Top each serving with the grated cheese, and as a final touch scatter the bell pepper, avocado, and olives over each. Serve with tortilla chips for dipping.

SERVES 6

TORTILLA CHILI PIE

Jalapeños are short, stubby, and dark green in appearance, and hot in flavor. Widely distributed, they are the most common source of extra heat for chili.

THIS RECIPE STRETCHES A MERE 2 CUPS OF LEFTOVER CHILI INTO A FAMILY-SIZED MEAL FOR SIX. MADE WITH ON-HAND INGREDIENTS, IT CAN BE ASSEMBLED IN MINUTES.

6 large flour tortillas
2 cups salsa
2 cups prepared chili
1 can (15-ounce) pinto beans, rinsed
1 can (4-ounce) chopped jalapeños
1 cup grated cheddar or soy cheese
½ cup corn chips, crushed coarse
Shredded lettuce, diced avocados, and chopped onion,
   as accompaniments

Preheat the oven to 350°F. Arrange three tortillas, overlapping slightly, in the bottom of a lightly oiled 10-inch baking dish or deep-dish pie plate. Spread half of the salsa over the tortillas. In a medium saucepan over medium heat, combine the chili, pinto beans, and jalapeños, and cook until heated through, about 5 minutes. Spread the chili mixture over the salsa layer in the baking dish, and cover with the remaining tortillas. Spread the remaining salsa on top of the tortillas, and sprinkle with the grated cheese and crushed corn chips. Place the baking dish in the oven, and bake for 20 minutes, or until it is heated through and the cheese is bubbly. Serve the pie hot, accompanied by small bowls of shredded lettuce, diced avocados, and chopped onion as toppings.

SERVES 6

CHILI-MACARONI BAKE

🍅 🍅 🍅

A VARIATION ON THE "CHILI-MAC" THAT IS POPULAR IN KANSAS CITY, THIS DISH COMBINES CHILI WITH EVERYONE'S FAVORITE, MACARONI AND CHEESE. VEGANS AND OTHERS WHO ESCHEW DAIRY PRODUCTS CAN MAKE THIS DISH WITH THE NON-DAIRY OPTIONS GIVEN.

2 tablespoons safflower oil
½ cup minced onion
2 tablespoons flour
2 cups heated milk or soy milk
1 teaspoon salt
⅛ teaspoon cayenne
1 pound elbow macaroni, cooked and drained
2 cups grated cheddar or soy cheese
3 cups prepared chili

Preheat the oven to 375°F. Lightly oil the bottom and sides of a 9" x 13" baking dish, and set aside.

Heat the oil in a medium saucepan over medium heat. Add the onions, cover, and cook 5 minutes. Stir in the flour, and cook 2 minutes, then lower the heat and slowly whisk in the milk. Continue to cook, stirring constantly, until the mixture thickens, about 2 minutes. Season with the salt and cayenne. Combine the sauce with the cooked pasta elbows and half of the grated cheese. Spoon the pasta mixture into the baking dish and spread the chili over it. Sprinkle the remaining grated cheese over the chili layer. Bake for 30 minutes, or until it is heated through and the cheese is bubbly.

SERVES 6

Chile Fact

🍅

Chile caribe refers to a coarse-ground chile or chile flakes.

POTATO-CHILI GRATIN

ALL THIS CASSEROLE NEEDS AS ACCOMPANIMENT IS A SALAD OR GREEN VEGETABLE FOR A SATISFYING DINNER. I PREFER YUKON GOLD POTATOES FOR THEIR BUTTERY, RICH FLAVOR, BUT ANOTHER VARIETY MAY BE SUBSTITUTED.

3 large Yukon Gold potatoes, sliced thin
1 large onion, sliced thin
1 can (4-ounce) green chiles, chopped
2 tablespoons water
1 teaspoon salt
1 teaspoon dried basil
1 teaspoon chili powder, commercial or homemade
　　(pages 7-8)
⅛ teaspoon cayenne
1 cup sour cream (dairy or non-dairy)
2 cups prepared chili
1 cup grated Monterey jack or soy cheese

Preheat the oven to 375°F. In a lightly oiled 9" x 13" baking dish, arrange alternating layers of the potatoes, onion, and chiles. Sprinkle with the water and the salt, basil, chili powder, and cayenne. Cover the dish and bake for 30 minutes, or until vegetables are tender. Remove the dish from the oven, and spread three layers over the potatoes: the sour cream, then the chili, and, finally, the grated cheese. Bake, uncovered, for 15 minutes longer, or until it is heated through and the cheese is bubbly.

SERVES 6

CHILI-STUFFED CHILES

THIS IS A VARIATION ON A CLASSIC CHILE DISH, STUFFED WHOLE CHILES, BUT WITH CHILI AS THE NONTRADITIONAL STUFFING. IN ANOTHER DEPARTURE FROM THE CLASSIC *CHILES RELLENOS*, THE CHILES IN THIS HEALTH-CONSCIOUS VERSION ARE NOT DIPPED IN BATTER, AND ARE BAKED, NOT FRIED.

8 whole green chiles, fresh or canned, seeded
2 cups prepared chili
1 cup salsa
1 cup sour cream (dairy or non-dairy)
Grated Monterey jack, cheddar, or soy cheese

Preheat the oven to 350°F. Cut a slit down the side of each chile, and stuff each with ¼ cup of the prepared chili. Arrange the stuffed chiles in a lightly oiled baking dish, and set aside. In a small bowl, combine the salsa and sour cream until well blended. Spread the sauce over the stuffed chiles, and sprinkle with the grated cheese. Bake for 30 minutes, or until the chiles are heated through and the cheese is bubbly. Serve over rice.

SERVES 4

COUSCOUS CHILI PIE

THIS CASSEROLE CAN BE ASSEMBLED IN ADVANCE AND POPPED INTO THE OVEN JUST BEFORE MEALTIME. WHILE IT BAKES, YOU CAN MAKE A SALAD, SET THE TABLE, AND, SUDDENLY, DINNER'S READY! I LIKE TO PUT OUT BOWLS OF SALSA AND SLICED BLACK OLIVES AS TOPPINGS.

2½ cups water or vegetable stock
2 cups couscous
2 cups grated Monterey jack or soy cheese
3 cups prepared chili
½ cup fine-minced onion
1 can (4-ounce) diced green chiles

Preheat the oven to 350°F. Lightly oil a 10-inch baking dish or deep-dish pie plate, and set aside.

Bring the water or stock to a boil in a medium saucepan. Stir in the couscous, cover, remove the pan from the heat, and allow the pan to sit, covered, for 5 minutes. Spread the couscous in the bottom of the baking dish. Sprinkle half the grated cheese over the couscous, then spread all of the chili over that. Top with the onion and diced chiles, and add a final layer of the remaining grated cheese. Bake for about 30 minutes, or until it is heated through and the cheese is bubbly. Let the pie stand for 5 minutes before serving.

SERVES 4 TO 6

CHILI TACOS

🍅 🍅 🍅

WHEN YOU USE LEFTOVER CHILI, THESE TACOS PRACTICALLY MAKE THEMSELVES. THIS RECIPE MAKES EIGHT TACOS, BUT I USUALLY ALLOW TWO PER PERSON.

1 tablespoon olive oil
1 cup chopped onion
2 jalapeños, seeded and minced
2 cups prepared chili
½ cup salsa
8 taco shells or tortillas
1½ cups grated cheddar or soy cheese
½ head of lettuce, shredded
2 tomatoes, diced

Heat the oil in a skillet over medium heat. Add the onion and jalapeños, cover, and cook until softened, about 5 minutes. Add the prepared chili and salsa, and cook 5 minutes to heat through, stirring occasionally. Spoon the chili mixture into warmed taco shells or tortillas, and sprinkle with the grated cheese, lettuce, and tomatoes.

SERVES 4

Chili Fact

The flavor of chili improves if prepared a day in advance. Chili also freezes well, so make enough for at least two meals, and then freeze the rest.

CHILI-STUFFED BELL PEPPERS

THE ZESTY FILLING MAKES A NICE CHANGE FROM TRADITIONAL STUFFED PEPPERS.

> *4 large green bell peppers*
> *2½ cups prepared chili*
> *1½ cups cooked rice*
> *1 cup grated Monterey jack or soy cheese*
> *1 cup tomato juice*
> *1 tablespoon cider vinegar*
> *1 tablespoon light brown sugar*
> *1 teaspoon chili powder, commercial or homemade*
>   *(pages 7-8)*

Preheat the oven to 350°F. Cut the tops off the peppers, and remove the seeds and membranes. Parboil the peppers in boiling water for 5 minutes, drain, and set aside.

In a medium bowl, combine the chili and rice until well mixed. Fill the pepper cavities with the chili mixture, and place the peppers upright in a baking dish. Sprinkle the peppers with the grated cheese, and set aside. In a small bowl, combine the tomato juice, vinegar, brown sugar, and chili powder until well blended. Pour the juice mixture into the bottom of the baking pan, and bake for 30 minutes.

SERVES 4

CHILI BURGERS

THIS IS A GREAT WAY TO TRANSFORM YOUR VEGGIE BURGERS INTO SOMETHING SPECIAL AND ADD FLAVOR AND PROTEIN, TOO.

2 tablespoons vegetable oil
1 cup chopped onion
6 veggie burgers
1 tablespoon chili powder, commercial or homemade
   (pages 7-8)
6 burger rolls
6 slices cheddar or soy cheese
2 cups prepared chili, warmed
Salsa, as accompaniment

Heat the oil in a large skillet over medium heat. Add the onion, cover, and cook until softened, about 5 minutes. Add the veggie burgers, and sprinkle each with the chili powder. Cook until browned on both sides and heated through. Set aside, and keep warm. Brown the rolls under the broiler, and arrange on serving plates. Place each burger on half a roll, top with a cheese slice, and spoon some chili over that. Cover each chili burger with the top of the roll, and serve immediately, with salsa on the side.

SERVES 6

CHILI DOGS IN PUFF PASTRY

THESE "CHILI DOGS *EN CROUTE*" ELEVATE AN EVERYDAY FAVORITE TO *HAUTE CUISINE* — WELL, ALMOST. ONE THING'S FOR SURE: THESE SOPHISTICATED "HOT DOGS WELLINGTON" TASTE DELICIOUS AND INVARIABLY BRING A SMILE TO WHOEVER EATS THEM. SERVE THEM ONLY ON YOUR BEST CHINA, OF COURSE. MANY BRANDS OF TOFU HOT DOGS ARE AVAILABLE IN NATURAL FOODS STORES AND IN MANY SUPERMARKETS.

1 frozen puff pastry sheet (9½" x 10")
4 tofu hot dogs
1 cup prepared chili
3 tablespoons prepared mustard
3 tablespoons fine-minced sweet onion

Preheat the oven to 425°F. Bring the puff pastry to room temperature, and spread it out on a lightly floured, flat surface. Roll it out to an 11" square, and make two diagonal cuts to create four equal triangles. In the center of each triangle, place one tofu hot dog, and one-quarter of the chili, the mustard, and the onion. Beginning at the short end of the triangle, roll up the pastry to enclose the hot dog and other ingredients, folding in the sides of the pastry to create a neat cylinder. Repeat this process with the remaining three hot dogs, and place them on a baking sheet. Bake for 20 minutes, or until puffed and golden.

SERVES 4

CHILI-STUFFED SQUASH

THE COMPLEMENTARY FLAVORS OF SPICY CHILI AND MELLOW SQUASH JOIN FORCES IN THIS HEARTY AND WHOLESOME ENTREE. WHILE THE RECIPE CALLS FOR BUTTERNUT SQUASH, OTHER WINTER SQUASHES WORK JUST AS WELL. IN FACT, IF YOU CAN FIND THE SWEET, ORANGE-FLESHED HOKKAIDO SQUASH, ALSO CALLED JAPANESE PUMPKIN, THEN YOU'RE IN FOR A SPECIAL TREAT.

1 medium butternut squash, or other winter squash,
    halved and seeded
1 tablespoon safflower oil
1 medium onion, minced
½ cup minced celery
1 jalapeño, seeded and minced
½ teaspoon salt
⅛ teaspoon cayenne
2 cups prepared chili
1 cup cooked rice

Preheat the oven to 350°F. Place the squash halves in a baking pan, cut side up, and set aside. Heat the oil in a large skillet over medium heat. Add the onion, celery, and jalapeño, cover, and cook until the onion is softened, about 5 minutes. Transfer the vegetable mixture to a large bowl, and add the salt, cayenne, chili, and rice, tossing well to combine. Fill the squash cavities with the stuffing. Add 1 inch of water to the baking pan, cover, and bake for 1 hour, or until the squash is tender.

SERVES 2

Chile Fact

Chiles left to ripen on the vine tend to be sweeter than their earlier-picked counterparts.

CHILI POLENTA CASSEROLE

THE NATURAL MARRIAGE OF CORNMEAL AND CHILI WILL MAKE THIS CASSEROLE A FAMILY FAVORITE. INSTANT POLENTA, AS WELL AS PACKAGED, COOKED POLENTA, IS AVAILABLE AT SPECIALTY FOODS STORES OR IN THE GOURMET SECTIONS OF MANY SUPERMARKETS IF YOU PREFER A QUICK AND EASY MEAL.

1 quart water
1½ teaspoons salt
1 tablespoon corn oil
1½ cups cornmeal
2½ cups prepared chili
1 cup salsa
2 cups grated mozzarella or soy cheese

Preheat the oven to 350°F. Lightly oil a 9" x 13" baking dish, and set aside.

In a large saucepan over high heat, stir together the water, salt, and oil, and bring to a boil. Lower the heat to medium, and gradually whisk in the cornmeal in small amounts, stirring constantly to avoid lumps. Cook, stirring constantly, until the polenta begins to pull away from the sides of the pot, about 20 minutes. Spread half of the polenta in the baking dish, and smooth the surface with a wet spatula. Spread the chili in a layer on top of the polenta. Spoon the remaining polenta over the chili, top with the salsa, and sprinkle with the grated cheese. Bake for 20 to 30 minutes, or until it is heated through and the cheese is bubbly.

SERVES 4

CHILI BURRITOS

THESE FLAVORFUL BURRITOS ARE A FAMILY FAVORITE. THEY CAN BE ASSEMBLED IN ADVANCE FOR A QUICK AND EASY SUPPER.

8 (8-inch) flour tortillas
3 cups homemade chili
2 cups grated Monterey jack or soy cheese
½ cup thin-sliced pickled jalapeños
Salsa (hot or mild), as accompaniment
Sour cream (regular or tofu), as accompaniment

Preheat the oven to 400°F. Place about ⅓ cup of the chili in the center of each tortilla, leaving a 2-inch border around the edges. Sprinkle each with ¼ cup of the grated cheese and top each with some of the jalapeños. Fold each side of the tortilla toward the center, and roll the ends over. Wrap the burrito tightly in foil. Place the burritos on a baking sheet, and bake for 10 to 12 minutes. Remove the foil from each, and serve with the salsa and sour cream as toppings.

SERVES 8

CHILI PIZZA

ADDITIONAL TOPPINGS CAN INCLUDE CHOPPED JALAPEÑOS, SLICED OLIVES, OR CHOPPED ONION.

Meatless: In Good Company

"I have no doubt that it is part of the destiny of the human race in its gradual development to leave off eating animals, as surely as the savage tribes have left off eating each other when they came into contact with the more civilized."

—HENRY DAVID THOREAU

1¼ teaspoons active dry yeast
Pinch of sugar
⅔ cup warm water
1½ cups all-purpose flour
½ teaspoon salt
2 tablespoons olive oil
2 cups prepared chili
1 cup grated Monterey jack or soy cheese

Dissolve the yeast and sugar in the water. In a food processor, mix the flour and salt in short pulses. Pour in the dissolved yeast while the machine is running, and pulse it on and off a few times until the mixture is crumbly. With the machine running, add the olive oil and process for a few more seconds. If the dough is too moist, add one or two more tablespoons of flour. Process until the dough forms a ball. Knead the dough ball with the blade for a little less than a minute. Place the dough in a large, lightly oiled mixing bowl, cover, and let it sit for 45 minutes, or until it doubles in size.

Preheat the oven to 450°F. Punch down the dough, knead it about 10 times, and flatten it into a circle about 14" in diameter. Stretch the dough onto a pizza pan or cookie sheet dusted with cornmeal. Spread the chili over the dough, sprinkle it with the grated cheese, and arrange any additional toppings over that. Place the pizza on the lowest oven rack, and bake for about 20 minutes, or until the crust is golden.

MAKES ONE 12" PIZZA

INDEX